# SEVERN WALKS

*Fishing at Upper Arley, Worcestershire*

# SEVERN WALKS

A collection of circular walks exploring the
countryside of Britain's longest river

by

David Hunter

Photographs by
David and Vera Hunter
Sketch Plans by
Vera Hunter

ⓒp

CICERONE PRESS
MILNTHORPE, CUMBRIA

ISBN No. 1 85284 164 8
© David Hunter
First published 1995

## ACKNOWLEDGEMENTS

*Acknowledgement is made of the considerable input in many aspects of the preparation of the book to Vera Hunter and to Peter Quy who shared some of my Gloucestershire adventures. Thanks are also due to the Forestry Commission for its co-operation in connection with the source of the Severn walk.*

## ADVICE TO READERS

Readers are advised that whilst every effort is taken by the author to ensure the accuracy of this guidebook, changes can occur which may affect the contents. A book of this nature with detailed descriptions and detailed maps is more prone to change than a more general guide. New fences and stiles appear, waymarking alters, there may be new buildings or eradication of old buildings. It is advisable to check locally on transport, accommodation, shops etc. but even rights of way can be altered, paths can be eradicated by landslip, forest clearances or changes of ownership. The publisher would welcome notes of any such changes.

Walking books by the same author:
*The Shropshire Hills* Cicerone Press
*Walking Down the Wye* Cicerone Press
*Walking Offa's Dyke Path* Cicerone Press

*Front Cover:* Walkers on High Rock, Bridgnorth

# CONTENTS

NOTE: All distances quoted are approximate.

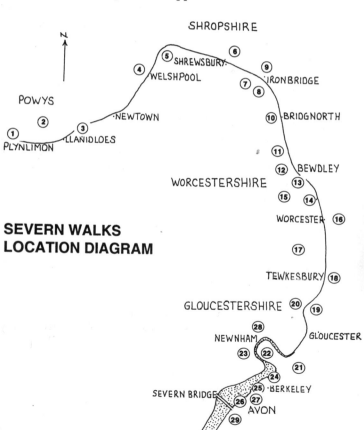

**SEVERN WALKS
LOCATION DIAGRAM**

# The River

The Severn is Britain's longest river and at one time was its busiest, carrying a great volume of traffic, and in favourable conditions was navigable to Pool Quay, just a few miles short of the Mid-Wales town of Welshpool.

The Severn, like its sister river the Wye which takes a much shorter route, rises high on the slopes of Plynlimon. It pursues a course that, with its many twists and turns ironed out, proves to be almost a half circle. It quickly gains strength, fed by the watery veins of scores of minor streams and, as progress is made, larger transfusions from substantial rivals. It is the mountains of Mid-Wales and the high ground of the Marches that dictate its course and make a contribution to the ground plan of the social, economic and political history of this interesting and sometimes undervalued, or perhaps more fairly, less well known area of Britain.

The first town on the river is Llanidloes with its half-timbered market hall dating back to 1609. From here the river flows north-eastwards via the well-kept village of Llandinam, Caersws, once a station for the Roman legions, and on to Newtown where the river sparkles to delightful effect as it tumbles over its rocky bed through Dolerw Park. Welshpool is the next town where the ancient Powis Castle looks out over the river valley with the Shropshire Union Canal sharing the way between the hills, albeit on a narrower and more disciplined course.

After a few miles the Severn swings eastwards under Breidden Hill, soon to leave its native land as it continues on a serpentine course into England. Its writhings soon threaten to lay siege to Shropshire's county town, Shrewsbury, which it all but encircles; seeking perhaps to extract a ransom from the rich merchants who flourished here for centuries on the wool trade. Now it veers away from the east as it makes its way towards the former East Shropshire coalfield that fuelled the industrial revolution of Coalbrookdale, passing under the world's first iron bridge. Here, channelled through a deep gorge, it flows steadily southwards to the cliff-top town of Bridgnorth and on to edge the Wyre Forest, crossing into Worcestershire and the Georgian architecture of Bewdley.

Onward then to Stourport, a town built to service the canal that linked the Severn with the Trent and Mersey Canal. Here the river has reached the limit of today's navigation with a series of deep locks keeping control of the river to Gloucester. But before that ancient city is reached, with its cathedral and historic docks, there is much more to be seen and enjoyed. Worcester, "the faithful city" with its civil war connections, has a world famous porcelain factory and the classic view of its red sandstone cathedral standing above the Severn, a backdrop so often featured in photographs from the County Cricket Ground.

Another bloody battle is recalled at Tewkesbury where rivals fought for the throne of England within sight of the great abbey, now regarded as one of our finest parish churches.

At Gloucester the wide deep-water canal cut from Sharpness provided a safer journey than the river and ensured the city's prosperity as an inland port. South of the city several places provide opportunities for viewing the famous Severn bore: Stonebench on the east bank and Minsterworth on the west are popular spots.

The river, now strongly tidal, widens with great sandbanks exposed at low water and distant views to the high ground of the Royal Forest of Dean to the west and the long grey line of the Cotswolds to the east. Here a castle in the Vale of Berkeley has the story of a horrific murder to tell, regicide no less. Between Aust and Beachley the Severn Bridge, built in 1966, with its 400ft-high towers makes an impressive crossing of the river. Thirty years on, the immense growth of road transport has brought about a second spanning of the turbulent waters, this time funded by private enterprise. A little beyond the bridge the Severn is joined by the Wye and the river opens out to its wide estuary and the Bristol Channel.

## WALKING OPPORTUNITIES

Unlike its rival the Thames, which now has a long-distance National Trail following its course from Thames Head to the capital, the Severn is not currently blessed with public rights of way throughout its length, particularly in its higher reaches. Further downstream there is more generous access to its banks, often with paths on, or near, both sides of the river. Herein may lie a trap for the walker intent on following the east bank and making a return by the west, if he has not taken the precaution of doing a little homework with the map before setting off, for there are places where the bridges may prove to be a mite too far apart.

The Thames has been described as "liquid history"; the Severn is scarcely less so in its contribution to our heritage. The walks that follow have been selected to provide varied scenic and historic interest.

While for the most part this book concentrates on country walks, exploration of the Severnside towns will be found rewarding. Shrewsbury and Gloucester are amongst those with town trail leaflets locally available. Many of the walks can be combined with visits to places of interest on or near the routes; a short list is included in the useful information section at the back of this book. In this connection readers are also recommended to make use of the invariably excellent services of local Tourist Information Offices with their expert knowledge and latest details on special events, opening times of museums and stately homes and accommodation.

No special equipment is required beyond the commonsense precautions of clothing to suit the weather and the provision of refreshments on the way. Stout footwear is recommended; although most of the paths are in reasonably good order some rough ground and mud will inevitably be encountered. Boots, while not always essential, will be welcome for their general comfort, ankle support and the security of improved foothold, especially in the rougher terrain indicated in some of the expeditions.

The sketch plans provided as an accompaniment to the text should not be regarded as a substitute for the invaluable Ordnance Survey maps, whose relevant sheet numbers are given in the opening detail for each walk. The use of these maps is strongly recommended for they will place the walker in the context of the countryside at large and assist in extending or shortening the recommended route, or finding alternative paths should the river be in flood. While great care has been taken in the preparation of this book the map may prove helpful in resolving any problems that may arise in interpreting the text.

Sadly, despite many improvements, our footpath network is still far from perfect with overgrown paths, stiles or bridges lacking, or impassably muddy due to poor drainage. Not a little retracing of steps has been necessary in compiling these walks and some routes have been abandoned as currently impractical for proper enjoyment. It is believed that the walks finally assembled are reasonably easy to follow, but it should be remembered that footpaths may be the subject of closure orders and temporary or permanent diversions which neither maps nor guidebooks can fully reflect.

## LONG-DISTANCE ROUTES

A long-distance path, Gloucestershire's Severn Way follows the east bank of the river for 50 miles from Tewkesbury to the Windbound Inn at Shepperdine, just over the border in Avon. A Severn Way, west bank path is currently in preparation but is unlikely to be completed for some time. The Offa's Dyke National Trail, a 168 mile route from Sedbury Cliffs on the Severn estuary to Prestatyn in North Wales, crosses the Severn near Welshpool. The Wychavon Way leaves the Severn at Holt Fleet making a 41 mile journey via the Vale of Evesham to the Cotswold town of Winchcombe. The Worcestershire Way is another regional path forming an attractive link between Kinver Edge and the Malvern Hills via the Severn, Abberley Hills and the Teme Valley. The Wye Valley Walk, a 112 mile route from Rhayader southwards, may be joined at Chepstow a little north of the M4 crossing of the Severn.

## PATH PROBLEMS

Any difficulties that may be encountered on rights of way, obstructions, vandalism of signs etc should be reported to the appropriate County Council viz:

Rights of Way Officer
Powys County Council
County Hall
Llandrindod Wells LD1 5LG
(01597 826000)

Rights of Way Officer
Shropshire County Council
Shire Hall
Abbey Foregate
Shrewsbury SY2 6ND
(01743 252363)

Rights of Way Officer
Hereford & Worcester County
   Council
County Hall
Spetchley Road
Worcester WR5 2NP
(01905 766877)

Rights of Way Officer
Gloucestershire County
   ' Council
County Hall
Gloucester
(01452 425000)

CAUTION

Winter walkers in particular are reminded that the Severn is a volatile river and subject at times to severe flooding. In these conditions it should be remembered that the water level can rise very rapidly. As I write Worcester County Cricket Ground is under 9ft of water, only the topmost rails of the racecourse can be seen and there are more swans swimming in the street south of the bridge than can be counted on the river proper. Riverside paths in town and country may be inundated and it should not be taken for granted that references in the text to floodbanks are necessarily an indication of a safe haven.

*The Hafren Forest from the waymarked walk to the
source of the Severn on Plynlimon*

# The Walks

## 1: IN SEARCH OF THE SOURCE -
### Hafren Forest and Plynlimon

*Start:*      The Forestry Commission's Hafren Forest picnic site found on the minor road 7 miles north-west of Llanidloes.

*Distance:*   7 miles approx. but see opening paragraphs for shorter alternatives.

*Detail:*     After a steady climb by forest ways the route emerges onto the wild moorland of Plynlimon to continue to the source of the Severn. The terrain is rough and wet in places although the return, mostly by forest roads is more comfortable. Boots are strongly recommended.

*Map:*        1:25,000 Pathfinder 928 (SN 88/98).
              1:50,000 Landranger Sheet 136 (Newtown) or 135 (Aberystwyth).

*Toilets:*    At picnic site.

The River Severn rises close to the 2,000ft contour on the wild, remote and inhospitable moorland kingdom of Plynlimon. The Forestry Commission has provided a well waymarked route through the Hafren Forest (ie. Severn Forest), which continues over the open hillside to the river's source. The best part of a day should be committed to this expedition, which those unaccustomed to hill walking may regard as hard going. An information board at the picnic site and leaflets (pay at the honesty box) provide details of this and shorter waymarked routes together with background information on the forest. For those wishing to undertake only the shortest of strolls there is a pleasant there-and-back walk to the cascades, less than a quarter of a mile from the picnic site.

This walk may be combined with a visit to the nearby Llyn Clywedog reservoir with its panoramic viewpoints and the Bryntail Mine Trail.

## THE HAFREN FOREST

The Forestry Commission was established by the government in 1919 to ensure an ongoing supply of home-produced timber. Thousands of acres of forest are expertly tended in all parts of the country, both coniferous and broad-leafed woodland. The Commission takes a great interest in wild-life conservation, providing many leisure opportunities with waymarked walks, campsites, orienteering trails and picnic areas. Public rights of way pass through many of the forests but in addition the welcoming attitude of the Commission allows access to its forest roads and tracks.

The Hafren Forest covers 3,000 hectares of mainly sitka and Norway spruce, larch and lodgepole pine. The forest, which was planted in the late 1930s, is now coming to maturity and is being progressively harvested, the timber being used in the construction industry for pallet wood, chipboard and paper. The forest is currently being redesigned; the management plan incorporates wildlife conservation, improvements in the layout to provide less sharp edges to the forest boundaries, more open areas and additional broadleaf plantations.

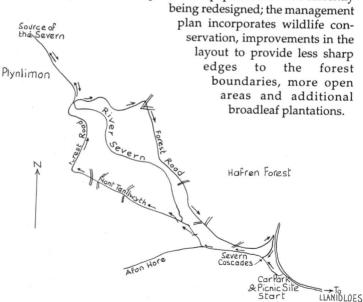

# 1. IN SEARCH OF THE SOURCE

## THE WALK

The waymarked routes are colour coded red, blue, and for this excursion to the source, white. The sometimes soggy ground along the riverside as far as the cascades has been defeated by the construction of a nicely engineered boarded walk, which makes this delightful spot accessible to all.

*From the picnic site join the cascades trail with a good path descending to the river to follow it upstream on the boardwalk crafted with the competence we have come to expect from the Forestry Commission's engineers.*

The infant river tumbles down a rocky staircase, the roar of the Severn over the cataract proclaiming its power like a young lion testing out the strength of its growing voice. Here the water runs clean and clear in contrast to the brown waters of the tidal reaches of the river's full maturity.

*From the cascades the path climbs a rocky step into the forest, still following the course of the Severn but without the benefit of the boardwalk. Soon a hut is passed where sensors measure the flow of the river between a concrete embankment.* A notice announces "Severn Flume. This structure measures the river discharge of the Severn. It is part of an intricate network installed to study the hydrology of the drainage basin upstream at this point... for further details contact Institute of Hydrology, Wallingford, Berks." The river's flow is not the only thing that is being carefully monitored for there are several meteorological stations and rain gauges set about the forest and the open mountain.

*Beyond the hut the path widens with a view ahead of the forest climbing the eastern slopes of Plynlimon. Buzzards may be seen soaring high above or closer to their nesting sites in the trees. Continue upstream between spruce trees on the clear stony track. Bend right with the Severn as the Afon Hore joins the mainstream. In about 100 yards cross the river by a footbridge and turn right to continue upstream with the river now in a deeper bed. From here on the wetter patches of the way have been made easier for the walker by the liberal scattering of forest bark, making its own intermittent trail augmenting the generously provided waymarked posts.*

The river along this section is still several feet wide but is briefly forced into a rocky channel only a foot wide, where it roars its defiance as it tunnels its way through.

*After 100 yards swing left, continuing to follow closely the white-painted waymarks that take you into the darkness of the forest. Immediately over a streamlet a short climb is soon reversed as the path descends to a river, not the Severn but the Nant Tanllwyth which is met by another flume and is followed upstream.*

*After about 200 yards turn right over a small wooden bridge across a rivulet and then left - there is a large arrowed sign, "Blaen Hafren Plynlimon".*

*The path, which is sometimes steep and slippery, runs north-westerly paralleling the course of the Nant Tanllwyth for nearly a mile, each twist and turn waymarked, with directional signs at the forest road crossings.* There are wide-ranging views as you look back over the vast green acres of the forest dipping and rising in great waves. Closer at hand the Tanllwyth provides its own entertainment as it rushes helter-skelter down the hillside.

*The uphill path is pursued until you meet the forest road running south from Carreg Wen, not far from the forest boundary. Turn right (north) again with some fine views over the forest. After a while a path is signed off to Plynlimon via Carreg Wen; ignore this and continue, signed Blaen Hafren. As you advance, the rounded height of Carn Biga is seen ahead rising above the forest. The road makes a sharp bend to the left with the sound of the Severn Falls carried up through the trees.*

*The road straightens out and pursues its northward course for 300 yards. Just as it makes a sharp curve to the right a white post marks a narrow path on the left, which follows the now tiny Severn stream for a short distance under trees to emerge onto the open hillside by way of a stile.*

*Keep to the waymarked path to the right and a little higher than the hollow which the Severn has carved for itself.* Here you are on a bare landscape of rough grass, rush and peaty moorland. In summer larks rise singing joyously above the heather where they have carefully concealed their nests. Away to your left the main summits of Plynlimon peak at 2,467 feet, and to the right the lesser hills of Carn Biga can be seen. It is a wild and lonely place with an austere beauty of its own, often with no sign of life save a scattering of sheep, white sails upon a rough green sea.

*It is almost three-quarters of a mile from the forest edge to the source of the river with the way becoming wetter under foot as the eroding face of the landscape sloughs off its top skin to reveal the black bare crumbling peat: when dry soft and springy, when wet a squelchy black porridge, often ankle deep. At last two stout posts announce the source, one carrying the legend in Welsh, the other in English.*

Any temptation to emulate the Victorian writer George Borrow, who made a point of sampling the headwaters of both the Severn and Wye, is easily resisted for the boggy pool from which the river starts its long journey is likely to have an appeal only for the desperately thirsty.

## THE RETURN ROUTE

*Having drunk your fill of the scenery, if not the spring, retrace your steps to the forest and on reaching the road turn left, signed Rhyd-y-Benwch. The return is almost entirely on forest roads and is waymarked back to the cascades.*

*Pursue the broad forest road as it winds downhill with a succession of long views over the forest and its great crop of timber. On meeting a junction of four forest roads, turn right and after about 150 yards the road again divides; turn left, still signed to Rhyd-y-Benwch. This is a long steady winding descent. After some distance a newish forest road rises to meet your way from diagonal right but continue with further minor forest roads coming in from right and left. About half a mile after your way has been joined by the blue waymarked route swing sharp diagonal right on a narrow forest road descending towards the Severn seen ahead. After 200 yards swing sharp left on the forest road (still signed Rhyd-y-Benwch) with the Severn on your right. After about 300 yards you will meet the flume first encountered on the outward journey; take the path through the short stretch of trees to the cascades and return to the picnic site by way of the boardwalk.*

## 2: BRYNTAIL AND CLYWEDOG

Start:          Bwlch-y-gle dam located on the B4518 3 miles north-west of
                Llanidloes.

Car Parking
and Toilets:    Right-hand side of the road with picnic site and information
                board.

Distance:       A linear walk - 4 miles there and back.

Detail:         A valley path rises to the road and follows Glyndwr's Way to
                the Clywedog Gorge and the former Bryntail Mine.

Maps:           1:25,000 Pathfinder 928 (SN 88/98).

                1:50,000 Landranger 136.

The car park looks over Llyn Clywedog, a reservoir covering 650 acres which was completed in 1967. A second and better viewpoint is found half a mile further on but the most spectacular is sited on the minor road set high above the south-western corner of the dam. In Walk 1 I mentioned the Bryntail Mine Trail and those wishing only to inspect the site and enjoy the wide prospect from the various viewpoints should take the B4518 from Llanidloes and turn left on the signed minor road which leads to the foot of the dam, the Clywedog Gorge and the former mine. A free leaflet published by Severn Trent Water describing a 20-40 minute trail is available from a box near the car park entrance. The viewpoint above the dam is reached by car in a few minutes and walkers opting for a lazy day can keep to the car to make a full scenic circuit of the great reservoir by the quiet lanes that lead to the oddly named village of Staylittle and back by the B4518 to complete the round.

The dam at the time of its opening held the record for the tallest dam in Britain at 235ft. Unlike the Elan Valley reservoirs and others the lake does not supply water by pipeline but was built to control the high rainfall levels of this part of Wales, holding back a huge volume of water to even out the river's flow. The release of water to the Afon Clywedog, which joins the Severn at Llanidloes, is carefully monitored to help reduce winter flooding and top up the river in drier periods. Water from Clywedog eventually finds its way into the homes of those who live in the West Midlands as Severn Trent

*Bryntail mine and the Clywedog Gorge*

Water draws supplies into subsidiary reservoirs further down the Severn.

The original intention of this walk had been to provide a circuit of 5 or 6 miles, visiting the old mining village of Fan then continuing to the Clywedog Gorge and the dam, with a return in part by Glyndwr's Way. However problems arose with footpath access, which are being examined by the County Council. If and when resolved the planned circuit should appear in future editions.

Glyndwr's Way is a 120 mile regional path from Knighton to Machynlleth, where the Welsh patriot is reputed to have held his Parliament, thence to Welshpool where a link is made with the Offa's Dyke Path. It is a wild but rewarding route. A set of leaflet guides is published by Powys County Council.

THE WALK

*From the Bwlch-y-gle picnic site take the descending metalled track. When after a short distance it divides, bear right on a curving path passing behind*

19

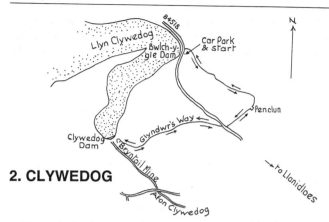

## 2. CLYWEDOG

*and beneath the picnic site. The track again divides at a gate; here turn left over a small bridge and then turn right to follow the path which runs close to a small stream.*

There is a strong touch of the wild here; to your left the 1,580ft-high bracken and heather-covered Bryn y Fan closes the valley and to your right beyond the stream a lesser but rugged hillside forms the second arm of the vice, with an ancient hill fort on its summit.

*After a quarter of a mile cross the stream and over a stile to turn left on a broad track and follow this for 200 yards. When this divides take the right rising fork with a view to the earth and stone-reinforced embankment used to provide a head of water during the valley's mining days. The Fan, further downstream, enjoyed intermittent periods of prosperity, heavily dependant on the demand and competitive prices for lead.*

*The track curves up the hillside to cross a bridge over the deep cleft worn by a stream before passing through the yard of Penclun and continues to meet the road, B4518.* The extensive view to your left includes the old mining village with its white-painted grey-slated houses and red-roofed barns, the tall chimney stacks in the quarry area and the black scarring of spoil heaps. More distantly there is a wide view to the hills with the 30 or so columns which form the wind farm above Llandinam. Further to the east the tall stone pillar of Rodney's column marks the Breidden Hills visited in a later walk.

*Cross the road to follow the signed Glyndwr's Way, which initially follows a metalled track to Bryntail Farm. Pass through the farmyard and continue along the signed way to a conifer plantation; here turn right, descending by a winding track to the foot of the dam and the ruined buildings of the Bryntail Mine.* On the map you will have already noted references to mines and shafts just south of Bryntail Farm and beyond Penclun, and even more in the area of the Van Mines.

Beneath the dam the waters of the Clywedog, released from their imprisonment, rush at a great pace under a footbridge beyond which lies the car park and a box with the trail leaflets.

The ruins are all that remain of a nineteenth-century processing mill used to crush the quarried stone and extract the valuable lead ore by water-powered machinery. An information board and the leaflet provide a brief but interesting history of the mine, which was at the height of its production in the mid-nineteenth century.

*Retrace the steps via Bryntail Farm to meet the road returning to the car park by the footpath taken on your outward journey or follow the roadside verge.*

# 3: LLANDINAM AND THE WINDS OF HEAVEN

| | |
|---|---|
| *Start:* | Disused quarry, south-east of Llandinam. The village lies 8 miles to the west of Newtown and is reached via the A489 and A470 Llanidloes road. Leave the A470 and take the single track gated road which, after a mile of ascent via Cobbler's Gate, ends at an abandoned quarry where there is space to leave a few cars. |
| *Distance:* | 4 miles. |
| *Detail:* | Lonely tracks climb to over 1,700ft, for the most part easy to follow but at one point disappearing for a while, so care is required in navigating some rough and sometimes wet grass-land. Boots recommended. |
| *Maps:* | 1:25,000 Pathfinder 929 (SO 08/18). |
| | 1:50,000 Landranger 136. |

Llandinam won the title "Best kept village in Wales 1985", an honour that would surely have delighted David Davies whose statue can be seen on the main road by the Severn bridge. He was born in a hillside cottage overlooking the village in 1818 and found employment in the local sawmill but soon launched into business on his own account. He became a railway contractor, mine owner and later built Barry Docks and served as Member of Parliament for Cardigan. Having prospered he built a fine house, Broneirion, just above the west bank of the Severn. It is said that he chose the site so that he could look over the valley to his childhood home and to the chapel which he loved. His descendants were generous benefactors to education, arts and health in Wales.

On the west side of the river, paths (from which there are good views of the valley and the Severn) lead to the remains of a hill fort, Y Gaer, set above the woods and fields, but our route makes for a higher, wilder country. The hills climb sharply from the floor of the valley. South-east of the village is the long ridge of Yr Allt Gethin (1,476ft), Moel Lart and beyond Bryn Gwyn, where radio masts point long fingers to the sky from a 1,500ft base. Masts apart, it is a timeless landscape, grazed by sheep for hundreds, probably thousands of years, rough grass, some greener pastures recovered from the bracken with rushes signalling the wetter areas and on the slopes of Bryn Gwyn, heather. Hidden from the village, it is a lost world vastly different from the neatly patterned fields of the Severn valley. Buzzards soar heavenward with enviable ease, crows and ravens find a living here too, the call of a curlew may be heard, and larks rise singing on the wind.

Some minor quarrying in the past and the need of farmers to reach their flocks have provided the walker with some good easy-to-follow tracks. Not that you are likely to be in any sort of a crowd for this is a lonely tract of countryside not yet discovered by those who follow the all too well-worn ways upon over-walked and over-publicised hills. You may indeed be completely alone save the brief glimpse of the black silhouette of a horse rider before it disappears over a distant ridge. At one point the way virtually vanishes; this should not present a problem on a clear day but if there is the possibility of being enveloped by low cloud the route is best avoided except by those with good navigational skills. There is in fact a track that can be used to shorten the route if necessary; attention is drawn to this later on.

"Timeless landscape" is not wholly correct, for a new aspect is being added even as this book is being written; a piece of modern technology advancing in the footsteps of an older science as the tall towers of a wind farm grow steadily on the hills.

THE WALK

*From the quarry the metalled lane becomes a rough track; follow this, ignoring the gated road half left. The way climbs steadily, turning southwards, and after just over 300 yards divides at a Y-junction. Take the left fork, passing sheep pens to your left. The track dips and rises and after 200 yards again divides. Here bear left over a bridge on the track which winds up the hillside, heading generally eastwards with Bryn Gwyn (1,339ft) to your left. The full length of the wireless masts with their attendant buildings come into view, an essential part of today's living, as were the signal towers and hill-top beacons of our forebears.*

*As you near the summit the path curves left and then right with some evidence of rock extraction. Ignore the good track beyond the fence line and swing southwards, still gaining height.*

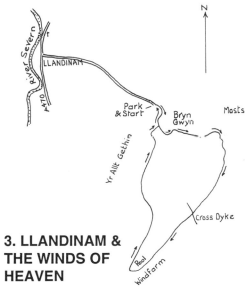

Now there is a fine view over a full half circle of the moorland, the mixed colours of grass, heather and bracken changing with the seasons. Through a dip in the hills you may glimpse the silvered thread of the Severn, the more verdant green of the lower hills in contrast with the blacker green of scattered plantations. The sharp eyed will pick out the little church at Llandinam with its

# 3. LLANDINAM & THE WINDS OF HEAVEN

short stumpy spire.

About 600 yards after turning your back on the masts, pass through a gateway. The track is more grassy now and bears slightly diagonally right, maintaining a south-westerly direction for the next mile. Soon after passing through the gate the higher ground to your left will reveal the Ordnance Survey's triangulation point (1,693ft). A further radio mast is seen in the distance and a gradual unfolding view of the tall towers of the wind farm, built in a great irregular circle above the headwaters of the Mochdre Brook.

The track descends very gently and about 700 yards from the last gate divides at a Y-junction. Ignore the left fork which heads downhill to the valley of the Mochdre and maintain your direction on the clear grassy track. After a few yards this passes through the small earthwork marked on the map as Cross Dyke. A few yards on and just off the track to the right, and easy to miss, is the so-called Giant's Grave, apparently the almost level remains of a round barrow, about 27 paces in circumference.

Shortly, a small feeding trough will be seen to the left of the track where a path crosses the way. Ignore this and continue. After 200 yards a clear track runs off right up the hillside. This too can be disregarded unless you wish to shorten the walk, in which case follow it up to the fence line to join a good track beyond it which will take you back to the starting point as later described. The junction is marked in the text thus **.

The track ahead becomes less obvious but maintain your south-westerly direction, dipping into a soggy area where a stream leaches out of the hillside, beyond which you pass through a gateway. The track now becomes so indistinct that at times it vanishes, but keep going with the rushy beds of the pool marked in blue on the map about 100 yards to your right and eventually the edge of the wind farm on your left. As I write this is still under construction with the tops of 30 or so towers all but disappearing into the clouds. Beyond the area of the pool turn sharp right, west, over rushy ground with the path now much more visible, soon to reach the fence line and a gate.

Beyond the gate turn right on a good track which keeps close company with the fence for the next half mile. A retrospective view along the ridge reveals the wind farm as a modern-day Druids' circle. **At a point where a track comes in from beyond a gate on the right (the short cut mentioned earlier) our route swings away from the fence to commence a long steady descent, a little east of north. An easy going enjoyable return.

24

The track shortly divides; take the left fork of the Y-junction (not very important for the tracks link up again).

Ignore the path which leaves the main track to climb the slopes of Yr Allt Gethin, continuing with your descent which will eventually bring you to a gateway. (Another gate ahead guards the path to the house at Waen-llwydion and a post carries a mailbox which closer inspection shows is a long way from its home environment, for it bears the legend "US Mail, approved by Postmaster General". It is a remote spot and one can only hope the postman has a van and not a bike.)

Our track turns right to descend to a further gateway beyond which lie the sheep pens passed on the outward journey. Bear left to return to your starting point after a quarter of a mile.

## 4: WELSHPOOL
### Montgomery Canal and Powis Castle

| | |
|---|---|
| *Start:* | Welshpool. |
| *Car Parking:* | Berriew Street adjacent to Gateway supermarket. |
| *Distance:* | 4 miles. |
| *Detail:* | Outward by quiet towpath and return through the parkland of Powis Castle. |
| *Maps:* | 1:25,000 Pathfinder 888 (SJ 20/30). 1:50,000 Landranger 126. |
| *Toilets:* | In car park. |

This walk passes both the Powysland Museum and the medieval Powis Castle; a visit to both is recommended. The museum, which incorporates the Montgomery Canal Centre, attractively presents the history of Montgomeryshire from Neolithic times to the twentieth century. The narrow Montgomery Canal, shown on your map as The Shropshire Union, linked Newtown, once famous for its Welsh flannel, with the Llangollen Canal. The canal ceased commercial operation over 60 years ago and, in common with so many other waterways, fell into serious disrepair.

Happily all is not lost, particularly for the walker; whilst not a

*Powis Castle, Welshpool*

definitive right of way, the towpath provides many miles of easy
peaceful walking on both sides of the border country of England
and Mid-Wales. Restoration work by canal societies in association
with British Waterways has been in progress since 1968 and it is

expected that the full 35 mile link will eventually be reopened to traffic. Picnic sites and access points are listed in a leaflet produced for the Montgomery Waterway Restoration Trust, a copy of which is available from the museum, housed in a restored warehouse on the Welshpool wharf.

The highly photogenic Powis Castle, otherwise known as the Red Castle for reasons which will become obvious, is now in the care of the National Trust. It occupies a commanding position looking over the Severn Valley and surrounded by fine parkland. Its attractions include a gallery devoted to the famous Clive of India, and fine terraced gardens.

Another local attraction is the Welshpool and Llanfair Light Railway, a narrow gauge line which operates in steam during the summer months.

## THE WALK

*From the car park return to Berriew Street and turn left to follow it to the crossroads. Turn right into Severn Street soon to reach the canal and the Powysland Museum (free admission). Cross the bridge, restored in 1900 at the personal cost of a local resident, Charles Nove, and turn right to join the towpath.*

*After passing the museum you meet the first very narrow lock, a tight squeeze only an inch or two wider than the long slender working boats. A made-to-measure job that must have been conceived with close attention given to the needs of water conservation, construction and maintenance costs.*

*Beyond a hump-backed bridge the towpath becomes a grassy way with an occasional swan drifting lazily on the still waters. Welshpool is soon left behind but the canal runs in parallel with the main road (A483).*

The Severn, half a mile to the east, is out of sight but there are views to the hills above Leighton Park. The Offa's Dyke Path, a National Trail, takes this line, bypassing Welshpool, before descending to Buttington, north-east of the town. From here, after a short flirtation with the Severn, it pursues the canal towpath to Pool Quay, then takes to the river again on a route that dodges some of the more serpentine writhings as it flows beneath Breidden Hill.

*In a little under a mile the canal seems to disappear underground; the bridge which carries the main road over the waterway with room below for*

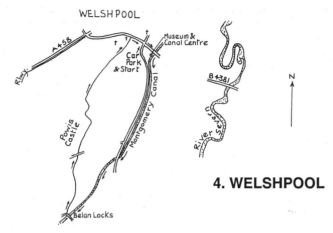

## 4. WELSHPOOL

the passage of canal traffic has been lowered to such an extent that only a gap of a few inches remains. This challenge to navigation is likely to defeat even the waterways equivalent of a limbo dancer, and one of the many problems still to be solved before the canal can be fully reopened for leisure cruising.

Cross the road and rejoin the towpath, now with even quieter waters as the canal draws away from the road, a fact not overlooked by Canada Geese who flock here to graze in the meadows in some numbers; I counted over 70 on one October morning. This season adds another dimension to the outing with the parkland trees and the wooded ridge above ablaze in their autumnal colouring. Swans too find this a quiet retreat for preening, setting a small fleet of white sailboats of discarded feathers adrift on the still waters.

After three-quarters of a mile you reach the restored Belan Lock with its picnic site and a "Canal Wildlife Information Board" erected by the Montgomery Trust for Nature Conservation; heron and kingfisher are promised the year round.

Continue to the bridge where there is a fine view of both the canal and the surrounding countryside, an excellent photo opportunity.

The towpath is now left to start the return journey. Cross the bridge and go through the gate found immediately on the right. Follow the climbing track that edges away from the canal, soon running under an avenue of trees, mostly oak and providing views of the wider landscape. At the top of the field pass through a gateway. The track is less visible for a while but head half left, crossing the field with a, possibly temporary, wire fence to your left. There is a view north-eastwards, to the distinctive shapes of the Breidden Hills, visited in the next walk.

The track heads towards a gateway where a bridge crosses a fast-flowing stream by a sheep fold. Beyond a second gate the track is again more obvious on the ground and is easily followed to the top of the rise to exit by a gate opposite the entrance to Powis Castle. (For opening times see useful information section.)

The rest of this walk is through the Powis Estate, not a public right of way but use of the main driveway is allowed. (Note there is a public footpath leading off the road 300 yards to the east.)

Go through the gateway and follow the tarmac road, passing the estate office and bothy, soon with the castle coming into view on your left.

Built in the thirteenth century its red sandstone blends with the autumn colours of the surrounding parkland; it is an impressive statement of strength with dignity. A magnificent wrought-iron gateway, topped by the heraldic griffons, offers a view into the splendid gardens with successive terraces laid out beneath the castle.

When the road divides bear right, signed Powis Castle and Gardens, making your way through the landscape parkland where deer graze beneath mature trees. Just beyond the Dairy Pond there is a small plaque which records the fall of an arrow shot by Sir Ralph Herbert from the Bowling Green - a powerful shot.

When the track again divides, if visiting the castle and gardens take the left but if not bear right and continue for three-quarters of a mile to leave the parkland by the lodge gates. Here go forward and turn right into the High Street, which leads on to Broad Street. At the crossroads, turn right to return to your starting point via Berriew Street.

# 5: RODNEY'S PILLAR -
## a view from the Breidden Hills

| | |
|---|---|
| *Start:* | Criggion, located on minor road, off the A458, 7 miles east of Welshpool. |
| *Car Parking:* | Space for a few cars will be found a short distance up the signed track at the forest edge. |
| *Distance:* | 2³/4 miles. |
| *Detail:* | A short but sometimes strenuous walk rewarded with wide-ranging views. Boots recommended. |
| *Maps:* | 1:25,000 Pathfinder 868 (SJ 21/31). |
| | 1:50,000 Landranger 126. |

In 1785 the gentlemen of Montgomeryshire determined to honour one of the great naval heroes of the day, Sir George Brydges Rodney. Joining the navy at the tender age of 13 his distinguished career, which spanned 50 years, took him from boy sailor to admiral with numerous successful actions against the Dutch, French and Spanish navies. It was agreed that the tribute to the great man should be a tall stone column set up where all could see it. As the walker will discover, a better location would have been hard to find; it is the 1,298ft-high summit of Breidden Hill.

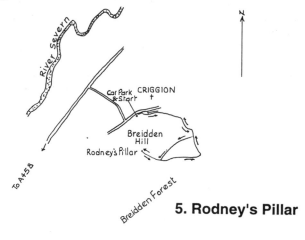

**5. Rodney's Pillar**

*Rodney's Pillar, Breidden Hill, near Criggion*

## THE WALK

Whilst there are some steepish climbs, this walk is easy to follow, the paths and bridleway through the Breidden Forest being exceptionally well waymarked. Most of the walk is sheltered by trees but the summit is bare and prey to all the winds that blow. The north-western corner of Breidden Hill is the site of extensive quarrying operations beyond which rise the tall masts of British Telecom's Criggion Radio.

The route to Rodney's Pillar is signed on the forest road found on the northern side of the hill close to Criggion church. Cars are only permitted as far as the parking space found a short way into the forest. *From the car park pass over the stile by a gateway and follow the broad track for half a mile, climbing steadily through the trees. As the track makes a sharp curve to the left take the signed path on the right soon passing a large boulder. Continue climbing to meet a bridleway going off to the left; ignore this and continue, heading south-west on a steepening path under*

31

*broadleaved trees. The remains of an old wall will be seen a little to your right.*

*In just over a quarter of a mile pass through a gateway into a more open area. Ignore the path immediately to your right and continue for 150 yards, taking the rising path on the right. The way divides after a short distance; take the slight diagonally left path and head for Rodney's craggy stone pillar which soon comes into full view.*

This high and windy hill top provides a superb viewpoint from which, as A.E.Houseman would have said, to look over "the coloured counties". It is a wide-ranging prospect to all points of the compass so that a large map and much time would be required to identify the countless hills that form the rim of a great circle around this pivotal point. Immediately to the south are the sister hills of Moel y Golfa, Middletown and Bulthy which suggest further opportunities for walks in this area. Many hills meld together to form the horizon of the southern arc. Picking out the separate components with a map flapping madly in a wind that is determined to snatch it from you may prove difficult; I confess to being forced to give up the uneven struggle. A list compiled in more comfortable circumstances includes excellent walking prospects spanning the Powys/Shropshire borders; the 15 mile Kerry Ridgeway part of the long trek taken by the Welsh drovers on their journey to the English markets; the wild Stiperstones; the heather clad Long Mynd; and Pontesbury Hill.

Below to the north the Severn takes a sinuous course through the mosaic patterning of the agricultural plain and there is a glimpse of its tributary, the River Vyrnwy. As the hills rise once more the sharp cut quarried face of Llanymynech Hill will be seen a few miles south of Oswestry. This is a place where a toposcope would be a welcome companion for the Ordnance Survey's triangulation pillar.

Ravens glide swiftly by the precipitous cliffs that formed the northern defences of the hill fort first established here in 800BC. The pillar has taken quite a hammering from the elements during its 200 plus years on this exposed hill top. The now difficult-to-read inscription on the west side of the column records repairs in 1849 and 1896; a further plaque on the eastern face notes work in 1983.

*Having drunk your fill of the 360 degree portrait of this border country,*

*Severn Cascades, Hafren Forest*

On the moors above Llandilam
Montgomeryshire Canal - Belan Locks near Welshpool

retrace your steps down the hill towards the forest. At the foot of the first descent, instead of turning left on the way you came, cross the stile opposite to the path which runs diagonally left, roughly eastwards. The steadily descending path opens out to give a view to your right of Middletown and Bulthy hills.

After about 600 yards you meet a bridle path at a T-junction. Turn left onto this, soon making a steep descent. After 300 yards you meet the route of your outward journey. Bear right, downhill, and on meeting the forest road turn left to retrace your steps to the car park.

# 6: HAUGHMOND HILL - forest walk with extensive views

| | |
|---|---|
| *Start:* | Haughmond Forest, 3 miles north-east of Shrewsbury. |
| *Car Parking:* | Forestry Commission facility, located on the minor road off the B5062. |
| *Distance:* | 3 miles. |
| *Detail:* | Mainly level walking on good paths with wide views. |
| *Maps:* | 1:25,000 Pathfinder 869 (SJ 41/51). 1:50,000 Landranger 126. |

It is not always the highest peaks that provide the best views, for often it is situation rather than stature that contributes to the quality of the prospect. Haughmond Hill is just such a spot. It is a little under the 500ft contour and yet the view from the south-western scarp belies its modest height, with half of Shropshire rolled out for your inspection. And not only an enormous relief map, for on one of those days when sun and racing clouds combine to selectively light the theatre of the landscape there may be an equally rewarding skyscape; riches indeed.

Maps are scarcely necessary for this walk but if you have them bring the adjoining Landranger sheet to help you identify the distant hills.

This short walk may be combined with a visit to the nearby Haughmond Abbey, where the substantial ruins of an Augustinian foundation are in the caring hands of English Heritage and is open

*Read all about it - Haughmond Forest*

throughout the year.

The Forestry Commission, in its usual thoughtful and efficient fashion, has provided not only a car park and two picnic sites but three waymarked walks. A blue-marked trail of just over two miles, a red trail of just under one and a half miles, and an all-ability trail suitable for wheelchairs etc. of nearly a mile. There are also separate trails for horses and cycles. Our suggested route, although longer, follows the blue trail for part of the outward leg and rejoins it at the viewpoint for the return so that detailed instructions are reduced to a minimum.

## THE WALK

All the Forestry Commission's trails start from the southern end of the car park with our way progressively shedding the yellow, red and blue trails before picking them up again in reverse order.

*From the notice board take the path half left, and follow the blue-marked*

# 6. HAUGHMOND HILL

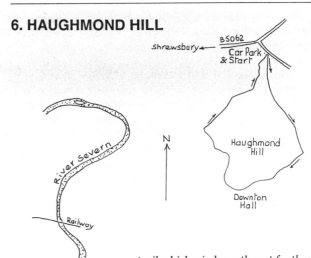

trail which winds south-east for three-quarters of a mile to join a track which runs along the inside edge of the forest boundary. After about 200 yards the blue and red routes should be abandoned as they take a sharp right turn back into the forest.

Continue along the edge of the wood, soon to reach a covered reservoir where you meet a stone chipping path. Turn left along this, descending to meet a Y-junction; take the right fork. The track soon leaves the wood at its south-eastern corner by a gateless gap; do not pursue it any further but take the turning on the right a few yards short of the wood exit.

Continue on the path which keeps close to the inside edge of the wood for half a mile, ignoring various unmapped paths which appear on the right. In late summer fungi will be seen, notably the bright red and highly poisonous fly agaric.

As you climb a small rise ignore the clear path to the right and continue on the slightly narrower way which runs along the hillside a little above Downton Hall, with a chestnut paling appearing on your left. Soon the path deserts the fence line and is joined by another coming in from the left. In a step or two bear right to climb the hillside.

Here the slopes have been left unforested and covered in tufted grass, bracken and gorse. Now is the time to enjoy the remarkably extensive views of the Shropshire hills spread in a full half circle, having a particularly dramatic quality when the long thin line is set darkly against the setting sun.

In the south-east, rising above the cultivated fields, is the steep and thickly forested summit of The Wrekin, 1,335ft high and with a hill fort dating from around 300BC. The steaming towers of the Buildwas Power Station signal Ironbridge and the Severn Gorge, with the long ridge of Wenlock Edge running south-west. Beyond the Edge rise the much mined Clee Hills, with Titterstone Clee Hill, (1,750ft) the highest point in Shropshire. Church Stretton lies hidden between the shapely Caer Carodoc, where some say Caractacus made his last stand against the Romans in AD48, and The Long Mynd. The folded landscape dips and rises again to the wild rocky spine of the Stiperstones, too distant for detail as it merges amongst its fellows.

Much nearer at hand lies Shrewsbury, Shropshire's county town, sited high above the almost encircling Severn. At least some of its features can be picked out with the naked eye, more with binoculars. You can see the dark spires of its ancient churches, the modern brick clock tower of the new market hall. Just to the left of the prominent concrete buildings of the Shire Hall the tall doric column that carries the 17ft-tall statue of Rowland Hill will be seen. Not Sir Rowland Hill, famous for the introduction of the penny post, but Lt. General Rowland Lord Hill, a soldier of great distinction whose battle honours include Corunna, Vittoria and Waterloo.

Behind Shrewsbury, 17 miles to the west of our viewpoint, is another prominent group of hills lying just over the border in Wales: Moel y Golfa, Middletown and Bulthy Hills, and behind them Breidden Hill with the stone column erected in 1785 to honour Admiral Lord Rodney.

*Having drunk your fill of the view from the promontory continue towards the forest to meet a broad crossing track. You have now rejoined the blue-waymarked trail; turn left along this. In a short distance a small loop turns left to a picnic site and another viewpoint. Our way, however, lies to the right, again following the blue-ringed posts which will return you to your starting point in about three-quarters of a mile.*

# 7: SHEINTON BROOK -
## old tracks and quiet lanes

| | |
|---|---|
| *Start:* | Buildwas, 700 yards south-west of Buildwas Bridge on the A4169 near Hill View Farm. |
| *Car Parking:* | No formal car parking. |
| *Distance:* | 7 miles. |
| *Detail:* | Lanes, field and woodland paths provide good views in rolling countryside. Autumn has the added bonus of its seasonal colouring. Some mud may be encountered. |
| *Maps:* | 1:25,000 Pathfinder 890 (SJ 60/70). |
| | 1:50,000 Landranger 127. |

This walk may be combined with a visit to the twelfth-century ruined Buildwas Abbey, now in the care of English Heritage and located immediately to the west of Buildwas Bridge. The new bridge, opened in 1992, is a successor to earlier bridges, notably Thomas Telford's first iron bridge built in 1796 during his appointment as surveyor of works for Shropshire.

This route includes some stretches of generally quiet lanes. Lanes are sometimes a neglected aspect of walking for those who feel they must be off the road as quickly as possible and road walking of any kind regarded as a tedious but necessary link to the next field path. These lesser highways can be rewarding in themselves, the confining hedgerows providing nesting sites for birds, banksides a home for small mammals, and the verges a wild flower habitat preserving species which may have been completely lost from the fields.

## THE WALK

*The walk starts close to Hill View Farm on the Much Wenlock Road to the south-west of Buildwas Bridge. Assuming you have approached from that direction take the good track on the right which provides a partial view of the abbey ruins. After passing Mill Farm, perched on the small hillock to your left, the lane curves and runs parallel with a dismantled railway. A little beyond the old railway lies the Severn; although close at hand*

*Sheinton Church*

it is usually invisible, hiding below the banks as it pursues a winding course. To the north the view over the hedges is to the narrow, but two miles long, forested height (1,335ft) of The Wrekin. Its isolated situation gives it a dominance over the landscape it would not in other circumstances enjoy. It is not by any means the highest point in Shropshire but is symbolic of the county as reflected in the toast "To all friends round the Wrekin". Wrekin Views might have been a better title for the walk, for this mini-mountain constantly reappears as the circuit progresses.

*The lane passes Park Farm, beyond which there is a much improved view of The Wrekin and the merest glimpse of the Severn. At the bottom of a slight slope ignore the gateway and continue along the lane, transformed into a grassy track between hedges. The track continues through Buildwas Park Wood with oak, sycamore, hazel, ash and beech. The old railway is now more visible on its embankment.*

The line, the Severn Valley Railway, dates from the mid-nineteenth century, originally designed to provide commercial and passenger services between Worcester and Shrewsbury. Today it is probably better known in a truncated form following its rescue and restoration in 1965 by the enterprising Severn Valley Railway Preservation Society. The line now runs in steam for the greater part of the year between Bridgnorth and Kidderminster.

The track can be soggy in places and "slots" in these and later woodlands suggest that deer may be present; almost certainly you will hear the mewing call of buzzards, a disappointing "song" for so handsome a bird.

*After a while the track climbs away from the railway, through Piner's Coppice, and after levelling out meets a metal gate/stile and the driveway to Buildwas Park. Turn right to follow the drive over a bridge, soon to reach a lane near Hill Top Farm - more Wrekin views! Turn right and follow the lane into and through Sheinton village.*

The first house you meet is Ridgmount, the former Sheinton Toll House, built to collect the fees from travellers using the turnpike constructed under an Act of Parliament of 1770.

Sheinton, a tiny village, has a neat little church with a squat black and white half-timbered tower watching over the houses and farms in its charge from a small hillock. The tower is in the style of several Herefordshire churches and is actually in that diocese. By the church wall is a Victorian letter box made by T.S.H.Hawkes of Birmingham. They did their work well, ensuring more than a hundred years of service, although the top of the box is beginning to crack under the stress of the wall above it.

*Continue along the village road to the bridge that crosses Sheinton Brook.*

Pause to take a quiet look over the parapet. Here the stream, soon to add its waters to the Severn, is quite fast flowing. Fish dart in the clear waters below and we caught a heron in the act of gulping down his catch. The shallow waters and a plentiful supply of fish beneath the shelter of overhanging trees make this a particularly good hunting ground for this patient fisherman.

*A little beyond the bridge turn left on the lane that runs past Brook Farm.*

A steady rise brings improving views over a rolling landscape: the ubiquitous Wrekin behind you, Wenlock Edge to the south-east,

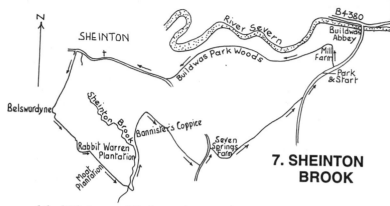

and the little tower of Sheinton church standing out like a lighthouse above the trees.

*At the top of the rise go forward, passing large barns on your right, to a crossing track. Here turn left following the boundary wall of Belswardyne Hall. The lane curves to the right. After a few yards swing left on the wide-hedged track which dips down to enter some woods, Slope's Coppice to the left, New Plantation to the right, passing reedy pools noisy with coot and wild duck.*

*Beyond the pools the right of way as shown on the map takes a south-easterly course through Rabbit Warren Plantation but this path may not be easy for the walker to follow so the landowner has kindly agreed to a simple alternative. Remain with the wide track climbing gently to meet a pair of gates. Go through the left gateway and turn immediately left to follow the outside edge of the wood for about 200 yards to rejoin the line of the right of way. Here turn right and head south-easterly over the field to meet the north-eastern end of Moat Plantation. Beyond a gate continue along the outside edge of the plantation. Maintain your direction (no visible path) over the field with a view to the long line of Wenlock Edge.* This narrow ridge, still quarried for its limestone, runs for 15 miles from Much Wenlock to Craven Arms. The poet A.E.Houseman knew it well and in *A Shropshire Lad* writes with great effect of the winds that sweep over this exposed landscape.

*Continue through the next field, descending to cross a brook by a footbridge. Now bear left along the bottom of the field to enter the broadleaf* woodland of Whitwell Coppice by a stile. From the stile go forward to cross a small stream by a plank bridge.

Here a stone retaining wall and a manmade slope suggests that in the past this stream may have been used as a source of power. Further upstream on the Harley Brook the name Mill Farm needs no explanation. Many of these small but often swift-flowing tributaries of the Severn were turned to good use for both agricultural and industrial purposes. Daniel's Mill just below Bridgnorth, open to the public, is one excellent working example.

Bear half right beyond the bridge to reach Sheinton Brook and follow it downstream for 300 yards on a narrow and, in places, slightly overgrown path. Leave the wood by a stile and maintain your direction, northwards, following marker posts to cross a field with Sheinton Manor to your right and a brick barn seen ahead.

Cross a stile, pass the barn on your right, going forward to enter Bannister's Coppice by a stile. Continue on the narrow climbing path through the broadleaved woodland of oak and ash with a ground cover of bramble and bracken. The edge of the wood is reached in a quarter of a mile; here swing right past a little green pond, still in the wood. After about 170 yards take the narrow path on the right found a few yards short of a stile on the wood edge to your left.

The path heads south-easterly through the wood for 600 yards, at first with some rhododendrons to your left. After a period of level walking the path descends through coppiced hazel to cross a stream by a plank bridge. A short slope leads to a stile and open field. There is no visible path here but head over the field to its far corner, passing restored cottages and conservatory beyond the fence on your right.

Leave the field by an almost hidden stile and continue with the hedge to your right to meet a road; here turn left almost immediately passing Penkridge Cottage. After 300 yards take the broad track on the right to pass Seven Springs Farm with its timber-framed barn and brick infilling. (More good views of The Wrekin.)

A short distance beyond the farm a crossing track is met. Turn left along this following the outside edge of a wood, in a north-easterly direction, and complete the walk as follows. In 200 yards the track divides. Ignore the left turn and go forward passing a ruined cottage on the left. The hard track now becomes a grassy hedged lane.

After 300 yards you meet two sets of gates. Take the right-hand gate

41

and continue forward, keeping to the field edge with hedge on your left. At the end of the field cross a stile and continue along the hedge line through a hilly field. At the end go over a wide waymarked stile, descending along the outside edge of a wood.

After about 100 yards turn left over a stile to follow a falling path through Brookshill Coppice. Leave the woodland by a stile and go forward with the hedge line on your right, shortly crossing a stream by a currently dilapidated footbridge. Cross a narrow width of field to a stile found to the left of a large gateway, and turn left on the road, A4169, to reach your starting point near Hill View Farm in roughly a quarter of a mile.

## 8: IRONBRIDGE AND BENTHALL EDGE

| | |
|---|---|
| *Start:* | South bank of River Severn. Ironbridge. |
| *Car Parking:* | Close to the bridge Toll House. |
| *Distance:* | 5 miles. |
| *Detail:* | Riverside followed by woodland paths that climb to Benthall Edge. |
| *Maps:* | 1:25,000 Pathfinder 890 (SJ 60/70). 1:50,000 Landranger 127. |
| *Toilets:* | Ironbridge to the right of the northern end of bridge and by the Visitor Centre car park en route. |
| *Refreshments:* | Various opportunities in Ironbridge. |

Ironbridge is often referred to as the birthplace of the industrial revolution, and with good reason. For it was at Coalbrookdale in 1709 that the Quaker ironmaster Abraham Darby discovered after many experiments the process of smelting iron using coke instead of charcoal. His pioneering work led to the production of iron on a larger scale than had hitherto been possible. His son, also Abraham, was mainly responsible for the construction of the world's first iron bridge which opened to traffic on 1 January 1781. Ironbridge and the nearby villages were once an immensely important centre of coal mining, brick and tile manufacture, pottery, and above all the iron industry.

Here the Severn flows through a deep wooded gorge cut by the

*The Wrekin from Benthall Edge Wood*

melt waters of the ice age. Once the river was said to be the busiest in the kingdom, with hundreds of trows and barges carrying raw materials and finished products up and downstream. Distribution was further improved with the construction of the Shropshire Union Canal and the Hay incline plane which allowed the movement of goods to and from the Severn into the growing network of the inland waterways system.

Time passed, the railway all but killed the river and canal traffic, and industry declined as production moved to other parts of the country. Dereliction laid a heavy hand upon the riverside wharves, the red fire in the kilns and furnaces turned to black ash and all was nearly lost. The rediscovery of Abraham Darby's early furnace led to an awakening of interest in the area. The Ironbridge Gorge Museum Trust has laboured mightily to create a complex of museums spread over several sites which present in an entertaining and informative manner the achievements of those pioneering days.

## THE WALK

*From the car park head towards the Toll House with its exhibition telling the story of the building of the iron bridge. In the early days it would have cost you a halfpenny to cross; even royalty was obliged to pay the toll. Now you may cross free of charge.*

*Once over the bridge turn left and follow the road upstream for just under half a mile to the visitor centre.* The remains of the Lincoln Hill lime kilns, an important part of iron production, will be seen on the right just before the centre is reached. If your time in this part of Shropshire does not allow for visits to the many museums of the area, at least spare half an hour or so to look in at the visitor centre to see the impressive scale model of the gorge and its industries as it was towards the close of the eighteenth century.

*By the museum turn left to the bottom of the car park, making your way to the river bank. Here turn right on the path which heads upstream.* Ahead on the wooded southern banks rise the four pink-tinted great cooling towers of the Buildwas Power Station dominating the landscape and much of our walk. It may be difficult to believe that these masterpieces of civil engineering are things of beauty but in their great strength of construction the vase-like shapes do manage to convey a delicate quality despite their huge mass.

*The path passes the Ironbridge Antique Centre to join a broad track which runs through the attractive gardens of the 15 acre Dale End Riverside Park. As the metalled path curves away from the river leave it to*

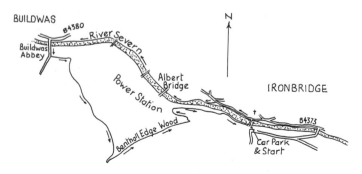

# 7. IRONBRIDGE AND BENTHALL EDGE

*take the grassy path that runs along the bank. The Ironbridge Rowing Clubhouse is seen just before the path passes under the Albert Edward Bridge, cast and erected in 1863 by the Coalbrookdale Company. Immediately beyond the bridge are the gardens of the Meadow Inn.*

*The path now narrows as it edges its way between the river and the fences of a row of houses. Continue to pass under the concrete bridge that leads to the power station, with pools of dappled light playing on its underside. Ahead will be seen a green metal bridge but the path comes to an end before this is reached and the river must be left for a while to follow the roadside pathway for about 300 yards.*

*Shortly after passing the entrance to Marnwood Hall the riverside path can be regained, descending a short flight of steps to pass under the green-painted bridge. A narrow rising and falling path is now pursued which emerges from the trees to follow the riverside edge of a field. Towards the field-end rejoin the road and turn left.*

*The virginia creeper-covered Bridge House now has an additional decoration, a slice of the Buildwas Bridge of 1905 replaced in 1992. Turn left over the bridge on the A4169 to pass the entrance to Buildwas Abbey.*

*After a short distance take the small lane on the left, found opposite Crossing Cottage, and follow this for three-quarters of a mile to the Pool View Caravan Park. The power station with its high chimney and cooling towers lies to your left.*

*Continue on the track, with a pylon making a giant waymarker as you head for Banghams Wood. The lower metal work of the pylon forms a framework for a view northwards to The Wrekin, a view that is immeasurably improved as you gain height and the dominance of the pylons is reduced.*

*Maintain your southerly direction through the woods until you reach an open field by a five-barred gate. Ignore the gateway and take the path over the stile to its right and continue on the hedged path which climbs to Benthall Edge Wood. Before entering the wood pause, turning to take in the northward view to The Wrekin, rising to 1335ft, not the tallest of the county's hills but probably its best known.*

*The track continues to climb through the wood and after about 300 yards divides. Ignore the grassy path that goes off to the right and stay on the main track which swings left to meet a gateway after just over 200 yards. (For future reference you may like to note that beyond the gate the track continues to Benthall Hall, a National Trust property.)*

*Just short of the gate take the narrower but clear path on the left. (A waymark soon indicates a further path which falls north-easterly through the wood.) Our way heads more easterly on a path which soon follows the edge of the north falling slopes, almost level with the rims of the cooling towers glimpsed through the trees to your left.*

Keep to the obvious path but when there is a definite division of ways go ahead on the left fork. The path again divides by a marker post carrying the number 11. Ignore the right turn and continue on the yellow-waymarked path that dips and rises to meet another waymark post - number 12. At this point, by a fence that guards an abandoned quarry, there is a long view through a window in the wood to Ironbridge and the former industrial villages above the northern bank of the gorge.

Turn left down a stepped path, then immediately right. After a short distance continue the descent on a long stepped path with railings which almost reverses your direction of travel before twisting back in the direction of the river. A junction of paths is met by a seat. Here turn right, climbing a little, now heading east with the Severn, largely hidden, below to your left. Views open out to the cottages on the slopes above the river and to Coalbrookdale church, where the channel swimmer Matthew Webb is remembered. A gradual descent is made, a plank bridge crossed followed by a stepped path.

When a further division of paths is met turn left on a wider track, then immediately right following the line of a now trackless railway. Shortly after passing under a brick bridge you meet the road, with the toll house to your left and the car park just ahead.

# 9: IRONBRIDGE AND LOAMHOLE DINGLE

| | |
|---|---|
| *Start:* | Dale End Park (car park near the Antiques Centre), Buildwas Road (B4380) found half a mile west of the iron bridge on the north bank of the Severn. |
| *Distance:* | 3 miles approx. |
| *Detail:* | Steady climb by field paths with a return through a delightful stretch of woodland close to a tumbling brook. |
| *Maps:* | 1:25,000 Pathfinder 890 (SJ 60/70). <br> 1:50,000 Landranger 127. |
| *Toilets:* | At Visitor Centre car park 200 yards in the direction of Ironbridge. |

*Ironbridge from the Iron Bridge*

This walk may be combined with a visit to one of the Ironbridge museums. The Museum of Iron and Rosehill, home of the famous Darby family, are close to the route, as is the Quaker burial ground.

Treasure-hunters have long been at work in Ironbridge and the surrounding villages, not in search of the romantic riches of gold or diamonds but the raw materials of industry: ironstone, coal, clay and lime. Drift mining into hillsides, the sinking of deep shafts, quarrying and the open cast extraction of coal have all been employed in the search for the great mineral wealth of the area. The abandoned workings have been reclaimed by nature but a thousand or so pits have been identified in the area. Walkers exploring the network of paths that climb the wooded slopes above the gorge will come across many such remains, limestone quarries or, as in this walk, the deep holes made in the extraction of loam.

## THE WALK

*From the car park return to the road, turning left towards Buildwas and after a short distance turn right on Strethill Road, a minor lane which leads to a level crossing of the twin track railway line that carries coal to the Buildwas power station. Beyond the line the road passes cottages, the tarmac giving way to a good hedged path. Beyond a gate the path continues on the inside edge of a small plantation with the remains of a pit in evidence.*

*After a short distance the path swings half left, climbing through a further small broadleaved plantation of oak and beech. The path emerges into the open to give a view to the impressive pink cooling towers and tall chimney stack of the power station rising from its wooded surrounds.* I had supposed that a reddish pigment had been incorporated in the concrete mix during construction to provide a lasting environmental match with the local red sandstone, but not so; the towers are in fact painted (most recently in 1991), the only ones in the country to receive this cosmetic treatment.

*Bear right, roughly northwards, to follow the hedgeline through fields for three-quarters of a mile with a final steepish slope to bring you to a narrow lane. Turn left and follow the lane for just under half a mile with views to the westward of the ubiquitous power station and the houses of Broseley climbing the wooded slopes of the gorge. Ahead will be seen The Wrekin, 1335ft, with its hill fort once occupied by the Cornovii, the Iron Age tribe whose territory spanned the middle Severn.*

*Take the metalled farm track on the right, found immediately before the lane crosses the deep cutting which accommodates the main road. The lane leads to Leasows Farm beyond which will be seen evidence of recent open-cast mining.*

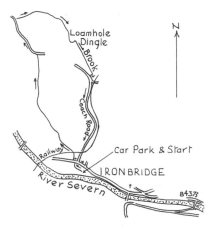

## 9. LOAMHOLE DINGLE

*A few yards short of the farmhouse take the path on the right through a white-painted iron gate. The footpath sign carries the buzzard logo of The Shropshire Way, a 172-mile route which takes in much of Shropshire's upland countryside. A detailed guide to the route is published by Management Update of Shrewsbury.*

*Head half left over the field (no visible path) to the stile set at the edge of a wood. Take the narrow falling path through the mixed woodland: sycamore, ash, beech and the occasional birch. A deep pit will be passed on your left from which the loam was extracted, now reclaimed by nature but the worn edges of the exposed sandstone suggest that it provides a mild climbing adventure for the locals.*

Here, deep in the hollow on a damp day with the trees still dripping on to the bramble and fern of the forest floor, the lone walker may feel he has unaccountably been transported to some distant tropical jungle. The balance is soon redressed when the sun breaks through with the dappled light and shade recreating the more familiar ambience of British woodland.

*The descent by the steepening path is assisted by steps which lead down towards the brook. At a T-junction turn right over a small culvert and after a few paces climb a stile and go forward on a wider path with fence to your left. The trees drop sharply down the hillside on your left with the sound of running water carried up from the deep cleft in the landscape, whilst to the right lie open fields. This upper path, marked on the map as Rope Walk, is followed for just under a quarter of a mile before turning left over a stile beyond which the path descends steeply to the valley bottom and the Loamhole Brook. Here and for most of the rest of the woodland walk the way is eased by the generous provision of steps and a boardwalk.*

*Cross the brook by a plank bridge with the path climbing again. At the top of the first rise turn right, soon descending once more. Maintain your direction southwards for 700 yards, a delightful way set under the trees and never far from the water's edge. As the brook widens turn right over a substantial wooden bridge which will bring you to the road near the railway arches.*

(Note that a little way up the road to the right is Rosehill, home of the Darby family and the Quaker burial ground.)

*Turn left and after a short distance right to follow the road, with the long succession of railway arches to your left beyond which lies the Museum of Iron located on the site of Abraham Darby's foundry. Here he spent long hours in perfecting his process of smelting iron by the use of coke instead of charcoal.*

*At the end of the road continue along the Coach Road, with the railway to your left beyond which lies the works of the Coalbrookdale Company, now part of the Glynwed group. On your right is Captain's Coppice where the charcoal burners skillfully turned wood into the vital fuel to smelt the ironstone before Darby's coke process became available.*

*Three-quarters of a mile of pleasant walking will bring you back to the Buildwas Road. Here turn left to return to the car park.*

## 10: BRIDGNORTH AND HIGH ROCK

| | |
|---|---|
| *Start:* | Bridgnorth town centre or from the Severn Street car park on eastern side of river. |
| *Distance:* | 3¹/₂ miles approx. |
| *Detail:* | Superb views of the Severn Valley |
| *Maps:* | 1:25,000 Pathfinder 911 (SO 69/79). 1:50,000 Landranger 138. |
| *Toilets:* | Town centre and close to Severn Street car park. |
| *Refreshments:* | Bridgnorth. |

Bridgnorth is really two towns, High Town on the west bank of the river standing on a sandstone cliff and Low Town which is now emulating its sister on the opposite bank with modern housing developments climbing the steep eastern slopes above the Severn. The town has a long history recalled by a series of architectural

*The sandstone caves that once housed a learned hermit, Bridgnorth*

bookmarks. The English Civil War took a dreadful toll of the town when a major part was burnt down following an explosion. What is left is the rich inheritance of a busy market town, approached from the north by the narrow and only remaining town gate. Beyond this "needle's eye" the main street widens to accommodate an unusual town hall, old inns and half-timbered buildings. Stepped alleys wind down the cliffside, and the remains of a great castle is tilted at a crazy gravity-defying angle close to the fine church designed by the great Thomas Telford. More will be discovered as our walk progresses.

## THE WALK

*The walk starts from the Town Hall in the centre of Bridgnorth but if it is a weekday you may find it more convenient to pick up the route from the Severn Street car park on the east side of the river and make a tour of the town on completion of the walk.*

The Town Hall has an out of the ordinary pedigree. Built in 1652 it is an inventive piece of recycling using timber from a barn brought from Much Wenlock. If open a visit is recommended, currently free admission and conducted tour. Its features of interest include a series of stained-glass portraits of monarchs associated with the town and the former assize court.

*Head down the main street with its old inns and half-timbered buildings. At the Cartway turn left and after 60 yards right into the narrow Castle Terrace to the Cliff Railway. The railway, dating from 1892, descends at an angle of 33 degrees and is unique in being the only inland railway of its type in Britain. The railway operates throughout the year but an alternative descent to the riverside can be made by a winding stone stairway. For the moment continue beyond the railway to take in the superb view over the Severn and perhaps to visit Telford's fine, clean cut St Mary's church behind which is the castle tower.*

*Retrace your steps and descend to the riverside by a long stone stairway or rail (return tickets issued). Cross the bridge and turn right along the riverside path, a favourite feeding ground for ducks and swans kept well nourished by the local residents. After about 100 yards, as you reach the footbridge to an island, turn left to meet the main road, A442, by the Severn Street car park.*

*Cross the road to the steps almost immediately opposite, signed as St Bernards Hill (about 60 yards south of the Fox Inn). Follow the broad flight of steps until they divide, then take the right fork and continue climbing to reach Morfe Road at its junction with The Mall.*

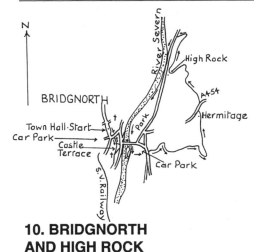

## 10. BRIDGNORTH AND HIGH ROCK

From the top of the steps there is a fine view back to Bridgnorth with the green-domed St Mary's church at the southern end of the town and the red sandstone tower of St Leonard's at the northern end. This is but the first of a succession of viewpoints that make this a particularly enjoyable walk.

*Cross Morfe Road and go forward on St Nicholas Road. At the T-junction turn left and then take the second on the right, Lodge Lane. After a short distance turn right into Birchlands and then left into Elmhurst.*

*At the end of Elmhurst mount the steps to a stile and cross a short field into Hermitage Wood. Pause here by the stile to look back once more to an even wider view which now includes the distant Clee Hills on the western horizon.*

*You are now confronted with several paths. The easiest way is to turn right and then swing left to reach the top of the hill. Here turn left and follow the path which runs along the inside edge of the wood, soon passing a covered reservoir and with views to the right over the Shropshire farmland.*

*About 200 yards from the reservoir take the path on the left which soon bears right to reach a triangulation point, a modest height just over 400ft but another fine view. Continue through the wood, heading northwards. When the path divides keep to the upper path which will bring you directly to the hermitage caves.*

The easily worked sandstone, a particular feature of the Severn Valley, has been carved into a series of chambers which in the tenth century were occupied by a well connected recluse, a learned brother of Athelstan, King of Mercia and Wessex, and grandson of

Alfred the Great. More recent visitors have demonstrated their erudition, but not their good sense, by the neat but unwanted carving of their initials in the rock.

*Continue from the caves, climbing a little before descending steeply to meet and cross the very busy main road. This is a dangerous crossing with fast traffic and restricted visibility.*

*The path climbs to the hill top where you swing left along the inside edge of a wood, mainly oak, beech and Scots pine. About 100 yards after passing a fenced-off and covered reservoir the path divides; take the left fork, currently waymarked.*

*The narrow but clear winding path falls and rises through the woods, shut off from the world at large, but in a few minutes brings you to the top of the high unfenced cliffs with a series of rocky viewpoints and a sheer drop to the road. This is High Rock with steps cut in the sandstone to an even higher bluff but for a more open view bear right along the cliff edge for a further 60 yards.*

Bridgnorth, with the distinctive towers of its two very different churches, lies downstream with the Clee Hills in the distance. To the north the Severn flows on a straightish course under the high wooded cliffs of Apley Terrace on its way south from the famous Ironbridge Gorge. Below is Fort Pendlestone, more military in name and architecture than in use. Look skywards, for buzzards are usually to be seen soaring on the thermals above the cliffs.

*From High Rock follow the narrow path northwards, terracing the hillside with a sharp fall to your left. After about 700 yards a wider path is met. Turn left on this, descending to meet the road. Turn left (towards Bridgnorth) on the roadside path under the sharp cut cliffs and passing Fort Pendlestone.*

*After 600 yards turn right into the park and follow the riverside path to return to Bridgnorth.*

*Ascend to the bridge by the steps by Captain John's restaurant.* Here a clock tower commemorates another piece of the town's history. The inscription reads:

"To the memory of two great engineers, Richard Trevithick, born 1771 died 1833, inventor of the high pressure steam engine, and John Urpeth Rastrick born 1780 died 1856, great railway engineer. Near this spot in Hazeldines foundry Rastrick built in 1808 to Trevithick's design the world's first passenger locomotive engine".

*Cross the bridge to return to the town either by the cliff railway, the stone steps or the Cartway. The Cartway route passes the handsome half-timbered Bishop Percy's House and as the road steepens the bricked up caves that were occupied as dwellings until 1856.*

# 11: UPPER ARLEY AND BEWDLEY CIRCUIT

| | |
|---|---|
| *Start:* | Upper Arley, off the A442, 3 miles north-west of Kidderminster. |
| *Car Parking:* | At the riverside turn right on a narrow road to reach the car park. |
| *Distance:* | 7 miles. |
| *Detail:* | Level walking on mainly good paths. |
| *Maps:* | 1:25,000 Pathfinder    932 (SO 68/78) (minute portion). 952 (SO 67/77) 1:50,000 Landranger 138. |
| *Toilets:* | Upper Arley and Bewdley. |
| *Refreshments:* | Upper Arley and Bewdley. |

There are good footpaths on both banks of the Severn between Upper Arley and Bewdley; this walk explores both. The Severn Valley Railway which runs between Kidderminster in Worcestershire and Bridgnorth in Shropshire keeps close company with the river. Arley station is located just beyond the west bank of the river; Bewdley station is about a quarter of a mile from Bewdley bridge on the eastern side of the river. As a rough guide the railway operates between March and November but not necessarily daily in the early and late part of the season. The opportunity may be taken to enjoy a nostalgic steam train trip by using the railway for the outward or return leg of this walk. A recorded timetable is available (24 hours) on Bewdley (01299) 401001.

Upper Arley is a small and pleasant village with a handsome red sandstone church set on a modest height which provides views over the Severn valley. The river makes its way downstream between well wooded banks and walkers may be rewarded with a glimpse of a kingfisher.

*Sailing on Trimpley Reservoir*

THE WALK

*From the car park make your way back to the village and by the footbridge take the path signed Worcestershire Way which heads downstream on the east bank of the river. At first the path is set well above the river but soon*

56

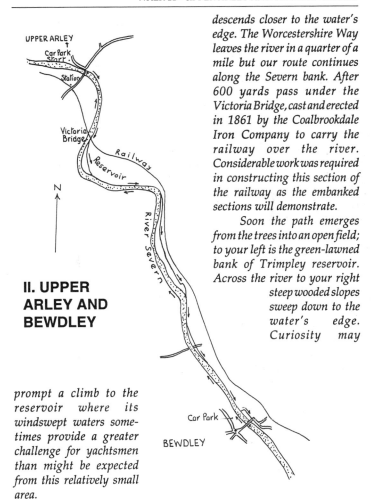

*descends closer to the water's edge. The Worcestershire Way leaves the river in a quarter of a mile but our route continues along the Severn bank. After 600 yards pass under the Victoria Bridge, cast and erected in 1861 by the Coalbrookdale Iron Company to carry the railway over the river. Considerable work was required in constructing this section of the railway as the embanked sections will demonstrate.*

*Soon the path emerges from the trees into an open field; to your left is the green-lawned bank of Trimpley reservoir. Across the river to your right steep wooded slopes sweep down to the water's edge. Curiosity may prompt a climb to the reservoir where its windswept waters sometimes provide a greater challenge for yachtsmen than might be expected from this relatively small area.*

Return to the river bank and continue downstream. The railway line is often hidden from view with only billowing smoke or a sudden shriek of a whistle to remind the walker of its presence. Train spotters may not be too disappointed for there are places where the railway runs very close to the path, allowing good photo opportunities for those patient enough to wait for the right moment or are in the right place at the right time.

*When a bridge which carries water pipes over the river is reached continue forward on a metalled lane which runs in parallel but away from the river with the railway embankment to your left. The lane is followed for nearly three-quarters of a mile, passing a long line of chalets to your right.*

*Just after passing a house called Bridewell take the path on the right to regain the river bank and follow this through a succession of fields and stiles.* The tall pillars of the bridge that once carried a branch line of the Severn Valley Railway westwards to join the main line at Woofferton still stand firmly anchored in the river bed, although the upper parts have been dismantled. *After three-quarters of a mile Bewdley Bridge is reached and crossed.* The Severn was first bridged here in 1447. The present structure is the work of Thomas Telford and opened to traffic in 1798.

The local museum in nearby Load Street provides an interesting insight into Bewdley's history and the industries that developed along the riverside and in the forest.

## RETURN ROUTE

*Even less explanation is required for the return to Arley. Simply descend the steps by the bridge to join the former wharf side which leads on to paths which faithfully follow the Severn back to your starting point. This section lies totally on the Worcestershire Way, a 39 mile scenic link between Kinver Edge on the Staffordshire border and the Malvern Hills.*

*The ancient Wyre Forest, extensive but nevertheless greatly reduced from its great medieval spread, is never far away. At one point the return route runs under the shade of the broadleaved trees of Seckley Wood, and some muddy patches may be encountered. The woods fall back before the Victoria Bridge, and from here the way continues to the box bridge that provides a pedestrians-only crossing back to Upper Arley.*

# 12: TWO PORTS OF CALL -
## Bewdley and Stourport

*Start:*  Bewdley, Worcestershire. Car parking on west of river north of Load Street or close to riverside at end of Severnside South.

*Distance:*  8¹/₂ miles approx.

*Detail:*  Downstream from Bewdley on west bank of the Severn, thence by Ribbesford Woods and Areley Kings to Stourport with a return via the east bank of the river, passing Blackstone Rock. Some hilly stretches.

*Maps:*  1:25,000 Pathfinder 952 (SO 67/77) and small portion of 953 (SO 87/97).
1:50,000 Landranger 138.

*Toilets:*  Bewdley and Stourport.

*Refreshments:*  Bewdley and Stourport.

Bewdley is a pleasant town, well known for its Georgian architecture but with a history that looks back far beyond that chapter in its story. One of a string of ports along the Severn, the nearby Wyre Forest was also a contributor to its economy. The entertaining museum in Load Street provides an interesting background to the life of both forest and river. Today's river activities include a thriving rowing club, raft racing and an annual coracle regatta. Beyond the east bank in the Wribbenhall district is the Bewdley station of the Severn Valley Railway.

## THE WALK

*From the car park located upstream of the bridge, head back to the town centre and turn left down Load Street. At the bridge turn right following Severnside South where the quay is stepped down to the river. Keep on the willow fringed bank, passing the cricket ground where a lofted six could well be lost in the Severn for ever, the cost of a new ball a modest charge for the joy of a mighty sweep out of the ground. Beyond the cricket ground will be seen the tree-covered sandstone cliff which must surely have once marked the wider bounds of the river. Comfrey grows in generous quantities along the Severn's edge, a plant for which the herbalists of old found many*

*Tax evasion - blocked up windows to avoid the window tax at Wribbenhall, Bewdley*

uses.

About three-quarters of a mile downstream from Bewdley Bridge, built by Thomas Telford in 1798, pass under the modern bridge which carries the bypass. Here the river curves past the high cliffs of Blackstone Rock on the

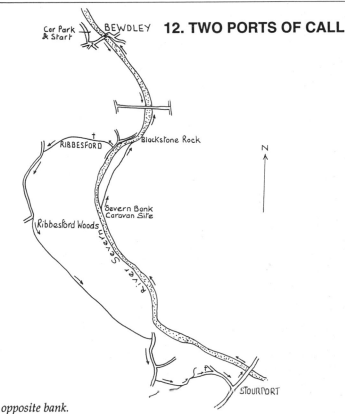

# 12. TWO PORTS OF CALL

*opposite bank.*

*A little beyond Blackstone Rock leave the riverside and turn left following the road for about 100 yards. Take the track on the right, signed Ribbesford Church, passing between an avenue of white-candled chestnut trees with the "onion" topped towers of Ribbesford House seen to your left.*

*At the church our route is joined by the Worcestershire Way, a 39 mile regional trail from Kinver Edge on the county boundary to the northern end of the Malvern Hills. A detailed guide is published by the Hereford & Worcester County Council and is available from Tourist Information Offices and bookshops in the area.*

*Turn left through the churchyard of the red sandstone St Leonard's church.* As you pass the porch note the now worn carving above the arch which is said to illustrate a rather tall story concerning a local huntsman who had the exceptional good luck to strike both a deer and a salmon with the same arrow.

*Continue on the path, through the churchyard, and at the top turn left over a stile. Take the climbing path along the field edge with the hedge on your right. At the top of the rise cross a stile to enter a wood but first pause to look back to the church and the view over the Severn Valley to Blackstone Rock.*

*Continue on the inside edge of the wood with an orchard, bright with blossom and daffodils in spring, on your right. In 300 yards leave the wood by a stile and cross a short field with a house to your right. A further stile is crossed to another patch of woodland, this time following the outside edge, and after a few steps continue on a metalled track, seasonally edged by wood anemone and celandine.*

*The track leads to a lane.* Here once stood the 500 year old Gospel Oak but only a stump remains. It appears substantial enough but beyond the first 6 inches it is a hollow shell. Inner decay led to its downfall during a storm on 25 January 1990, its epitaph thoughtfully carved into the short trunk.

*Turn left along the quiet tree-shaded lane. When the road divides after about 350 yards, forsake the Worcestershire Way which goes off to the right and take the left fork, passing Horsehill Farm on your left. From the lane there are views over Ribbesford Woods, the Severn Valley, the famous old carpet town of Kidderminster and to the outskirts of Stourport.*

*As you reach Glebe Cottage leave the road which now curves sharply to the right. Go forward to a gateway to enter the wood with a Forestry Commission board bearing the legend "Wyre Forest, Ribbesford Wood", a mix of conifer and broadleaved trees.*

*Take the wide track which runs south for about 250 yards close to the forest boundary. The path then curves left, heading south-easterly, for well over half a mile. Stick with it, ignoring all left and right turns. Leave the wood by a metal gateway, still with your general direction south-easterly.*

*The path follows the hedgeline, on the right, with the 407ft-high Stagborough Hill seen to your left. When the track passes through a gateway leave it and continue forward, descending in parallel with the track which lies beyond the fence. At the bottom of the field take the path half left through trees and over a field to meet the road (B4194).*

*Turn right following the road for just over a quarter of a mile, passing Coney Green Farm. Ignore the lane on the left and 200 yards beyond it take the path on the left. Head straight across a field to reach the willow-edged Burnthorne Brook. Swing left along the stream with the handsome red sandstone church of Areley Kings seen ahead on the hill and with Broomy Hill to your left.*

*When this great field through which you are passing has been freshly ploughed the red earth offers a striking contrast with the green hill from which the church looks over its parish. The path crosses a culvert and beyond a kissing gate turn left, and then up the hillside with the hedge on your left. Leave by a further kissing gate at the top of the hill by the church. This is St Bartholomew's, Areley Kings. The peaceful churchyard, with seats, provides a splendid view (more than a half circle) of the rolling Worcestershire countryside. It is a mix of plough, pasture and woodland, its hills rising up from the boat-lined moorings of the Severn.*

*On leaving the churchyard turn left, passing the ancient, jettied half-timbered church house, descending the hill to meet the road. Turn right, passing Areley Hall, and finally turn left to cross the Severn Bridge into Stourport.*

Here there is a sudden metamorphosis as country becomes town. Stourport developed as a riverside town much later than Bewdley and owes its existence to the canal age and in particular to the Staffordshire and Worcestershire Canal, a 46 mile "cut" that linked the Severn Navigation with the Trent and Mersey Canal a few miles to the east of Stafford. Its days as a commercial waterway are now past but as a diversion to the canal basin will testify that it is now enjoying a new lease of life as pleasure boats lock their way through the countryside of the West Midlands.

*The return to Bewdley is now made by the east bank, following the river upstream through a park with a succession of moorings. A large notice announces the upper limit of the Severn Navigation with our way following field paths close to the river with hills rising quite sharply from the west bank. Strangely, the eerie cry of the peacocks at Lickhill Manor are answered from the woods on the opposite bank by the equally unmusical call of pheasants, handsome birds for whom the phrase fine feathered must surely have been invented, if only for the male of the species.*

*Stagborough Hill, on the west bank, is passed and just under two miles from Stourport the path goes along the riverside edge of the Severn Bank* caravan park with notices requesting walkers to keep to the towpath. Leave Severn Bank by a stile where the river is also abandoned for a while. Bear half right to take the path that runs between a bank and lower ground to your left which accommodates a pond, much extended in winter, the willow trees spending much of that season with their feet in water.

Beyond the pool maintain your direction with the fence line now a few yards to your left and the faintly oriental topped tower of Ribbesford House coming into view. Soon the fence closes in and the walker is funnelled into woodland. Ignore the first stile on the left and continue along the clear path on the inside edge of the wood.

Leave the wood when a second stile is reached and continue along the outside edge of the wood on an improving track with the cliff face of Blackstone Rock to your right. The track rises to pass through a gap in the rock as it thrusts a nose into the Severn, the bright orange sandstone on your right providing a splash of colour in contrast to the dark weathered rock on your left.

The track descends to a gate and stile and on past another gateway to continue along the riverside path. The hermitage can be seen from our path, a substantial cave carved out of the easily worked rock where jackdaws whirr in noisy dispute and buzzards circle high above the 100ft-high bluff. The cave that long ago gave shelter to a learned recluse served another purpose during the Second World War when a local porcelain factory used the caves as a safe storage place for its dies.

The riverside path passes under the bridge of the bypass and on until it meets the road a little short of Bewdley Bridge. Note the timber-framed house on the east side dated 1623. Cross the bridge with its view of the town and the old quays and return to your starting point.

# 13: THE REDSTONE ROCK HERMITAGE

| | |
|---|---|
| *Start:* | Stourport. |
| *Car Park:* | East side of river access from Raven Street or more comfortably from New Street. |
| *Maps:* | 1:25,000 Pathfinder 953 (SO 87/97) edge only. 974 (SO 86/96). |
| | 1:50,000 Landranger Sheet 138. |

Rodneys Pillar, Breidden Hill, Criggion
The Iron Bridge

| | |
|---|---|
| *Distance:* | 7 miles approx. |
| *Detail:* | Riverside, field and forest on mainly good paths, two short climbs but no real hard work. |
| *Refreshments:* | Stourport and Hampstall. |
| *Toilets:* | Riverside park, Stourport. |

Stourport is a child of the canal age, conceived to service the needs of traffic passing between the Severn and the rest of the Midlands via the Staffordshire and Worcester Canal. The commercial trade has long since deserted the waterways but the canal continues to operate as an important part of the leisure network, a scenic link between the Trent and Mersey and the Severn Navigation.

Steamer trips ply on the Severn during the summer months, a well ordered riverside park has excellent play facilities, and south of the bridge "all the fun of the fair" is on offer. On a fine summer weekend Stourport is a lively place fully justifying its second career as an inland resort. The best of both worlds may be enjoyed with some excellent footpaths which take the walker to quieter reaches of the river and the adjacent countryside.

## THE WALK

*From the car park make for the bridge, climbing the iron spiral staircase and turn right to cross the river. Descend by the steps on the far side and turn under the bridge, built in 1870, to head downstream. The view to the east bank includes the colourful hurly-burly of the fairground and the Tontine Inn which overlooks both canal and river. Continue along the riverside path, here decorated with Himalayan balsam. A caravan park is passed to your right and when a further site is reached the path crosses a concrete "bridge" over a small brook.*

*The path remains faithful to the river until Redstone Rock is reached in just under a mile from the bridge. Here the cliff effectively prevents further progress with the path literally disappearing into the river when it is in flood.*

*Turn right on the path which runs under the cliff, where the easily worked sandstone has been excavated to provide a series of chambers believed to have originated as a twelfth-century hermitage. With care, and*

*The bridge over the Severn from Castle Walk, Bridgnorth*

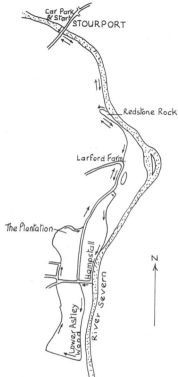

at your own risk of course, an exploration of the rock dwellings is practical. A closer inspection reveals a passage with "rooms" running off; one has a large chimney, a recess in the wall suggests a place for a bed, and small alcoves perhaps storage space for kitchen utensils.

*From the hermitage rock take the steps which climb the cliff and at the top turn left along the path, which soon provides a loftier view of the river. Swing downstream with the path which soon widens into a good track with a ribbon of trees along the cliff edge to your left and open fields to your right.*

*At the end of the field go forward between fence and hedgerow to cross a stile.* Here rough ground displays a generous crop of evening primrose, a plant now much in fashion in the world of alternative medicine for its oil used for massage and the treatment of pre-menstrual tension. Not, however, one that found a place in Nicholas

## 13. THE REDSTONE ROCK HERMITAGE

Culpepper's herbal pharmacy, and for good reason since it was a garden flower introduced from America, a common escapee which flourishes on waste ground.

*The track meets a minor road by Larford Farm. Here turn left and follow the road for a little under a quarter of a mile. A recently excavated private fishery is fast becoming naturalised and has been colonised by wild fowl. Their numbers include a small armada of white-billed coots, a pair of swans, gulls, a Canada goose or two and the ubiquitous mallard.*

*Beyond the pond, at a curve in the lane, take the path on the left over*

*Redstone Hermitage, Stourport*

a stile and head towards the wood seen ahead. Ignore the first gate on the left and continue along the hedge line (on your left). To the right are the substantial but now semi-derelict buildings of Seedgreen Park.

Cross the stile found on your left and go forward on a narrow path between trees. To your right is a deep overgrown hollow, thick with collapsed willows, once a pool but now looking rather bluer on the map than on the ground.

At the end of the pond bear left over a stile as you are faced with exposed sandstone by a misshapen tree. Pursue the path with cliff and hedge to your right. After a few yards cross the stile on the right and continue along the inside edge of a wood. Exit from the wooded area by a stile and turn half left to reach the river bank; here turn right, downstream.

Here the Severn follows a straightish course. The sharp rise to higher ground which lies back from the river seems to confirm that once the Severn ran both wider and deeper as the great melt waters of the retreating Ice Age ploughed a furrow through the soft rock.

After a while a stile is crossed to pass some mobile homes and through the car park of the Hampstall Inn to meet a lane. Keep to the lane through the riverside hamlet, soon passing a notice which announces Astley Public Loading Wharf, a relic of the days of the river's commercial traffic and the point where the ferry made a landing.

Continue along the lane, passing some attractive houses, both old and new. In 250 yards take the bridleway signed off left, found just beyond the telephone box and the village notice board, with a timetable for the once-a-week bus service to Stourport and an appeal for tree wardens.

The bridle path is followed southwards for a little under three-quarters of a mile. Soon after joining the path Jacob's sheep may be seen in an enclosure on your right, the ram looking particularly handsome with his curved horns.

The track narrows a little after passing a farm and continues through woodland. After passing through a gateway there is open ground to your left and the slopes of Lower Astley Wood on the right. At the end of the field pass through a gateway to bear right as the track turns westward up the valley, still with the wood to your right and a long fenced field to the left. Beyond the field, hidden beneath trees, is Dick Brook which edges the Forestry Commission's Shrawley Wood.

After about 600 yards, a little short of the end of the field, take the path over a stile on your right. The path climbs through the wood to emerge into a large open field. Turn right along the field edge and after 60 yards turn left on the path up the slope to the top corner of Lower Astley Wood, with its mature sweet chestnut trees overhanging the path.

Here there is a fine view of the pleasant rolling Worcestershire countryside, field and forest, the picture made complete when clouds bank high over the distant hills that fill in the horizon. But for the reddish colour of the soil you might for a moment imagine you were on the Sussex downs.

Maintain your direction on the descending path on the outside edge of the wood. As the wood falls back there are views to the east over the valley of the Severn; of the river itself there is no sign for it is hidden deep in the folds of the land.

Continue along the track which climbs to the hedge line; here leave it to turn left to meet and cross a stile after a short distance. Once over the stile turn left along the hedgerow for a few yards, soon descending between the cleavage of the rounded contours of the field to meet and cross a stile, a brook and another stile. Cross the short width of field to a lane.

*Turn right along the lane and after 90 yards turn left; when it divides after about 100 yards bear right. The lane climbs in a hollow with the red sandstone showing through a vegetative veil. Another junction is reached in about 200 yards by the Astley Burf Outdoor Education Centre run by the Borough of Dudley. Here continue along the bridlepath known as Scots Lane.*

*This lane is now followed past houses and onwards as it makes a half circle round the wooded area, simply named as The Plantation, with good views over the surrounding countryside. Towards the end of the lane there is a fine thatched house, complete with thatch bird on the ridge.*

*On reaching the road, which is unusually quiet, turn left, following it northwards for over half a mile. Seedgreen Park is passed on your right, the rusted corrugated-iron roofing of the lean-to barns a deeper red than the older brickwork of the main building.*

*When Larford Farm is met leave the road to retrace the steps of your outward journey via Redstone Rock and the riverside back to Stourbridge.*

This return over ground previously covered was not the original intention of this walk. One of the important paths on the route as first planned to the north-west of the Plantation proved to have a short, low lying section with poor drainage which after wet weather turned the stile crossing into a quagmire that even wellies were unlikely to overcome!

## 14: HOLT FLEET AND OMBERSLEY

| | |
|---|---|
| *Start:* | Severn Bridge, Holt Fleet, on the A4133 west of Ombersley. Car parking informal and probably unofficial but there is space at the end of the narrow lane to the right of the eastern end of the bridge. |
| *Distance:* | 4³/₄ miles. |
| *Detail:* | Mostly easy walking by riverside, field paths and lanes linked by A449. |
| *Maps:* | 1:25,000 Pathfinder 974 (SO 86/96). 1:50,000 Landranger 138. |
| *Refreshments:* | Licensed restaurant at Holt Fleet by start and PH over bridge and at Ombersley. |

*The Kings Arms, Ombersley*

This walk is also the starting point for the Wychavon Way, a 41 mile regional path which links with the Cotswold Way at Winchcombe in Gloucestershire. Coincidentally, our walk follows some of the paths of the long-distance route which is waymarked using arrows and a crown-like W logo. A detailed guide was published by Wychavon District Council in 1982 and should be available locally or direct from the council at 37 High Street, Pershore, Worcs.

\*\*\* A public enquiry is to be held into the revision of the footpath network in the parish of Ombersley. It is not thought that this route will be affected but walkers should take note of any diversions that may be posted.

THE WALK

*Take the path under the single span iron bridge supported by sandstone abutments. The path is followed downstream for a mile and three-quarters*

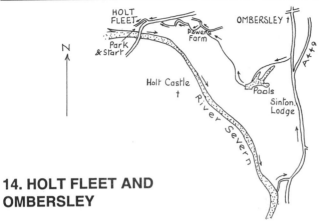

# 14. HOLT FLEET AND OMBERSLEY

*so that once the map has been initially consulted it can be put away for a while and the time devoted to the enjoyment of the riverside and its attendant scenery.*

The river itself is busy in the holiday months with narrowboats and cruisers, perhaps heading upstream to join the Staffordshire and Worcester Canal at Stourport which marks the limit of the Severn Navigation. Downriver the choices are wider. After 6 miles, having passed the cathedral, the narrow Worcester and Birmingham Canal can be joined at Diglis. Tewkesbury offers the opportunity to cruise Shakespeare's Avon to Stratford and beyond. If the charms of the Severn are such that the river cannot be deserted it may be pursued for a further 13 miles to Gloucester, an inland port with a long history. Even this is not the limit, for the attractively restored docks with their National Waterways Museum give access to the 16-mile deep water Gloucester and Sharpness Canal.

The tall policeman's helmet, more respectively named Himalayan Balsam, is found along the banks together with the smaller, pale yellow flowered toadflax and that other riverside plant with its large broad leaves and flowers that may be white, mauve or pink, comfrey. Fine cattle graze these fields with sheep on the higher ground to the west. The harsh cry of a pheasant may be heard from the long bank of woodland on your left.

As you progress the towers of Holt church and castle will be seen high on the ridge to the right. The castle site is believed to have been occupied for fully a thousand years. The tower dates from the fourteenth century; its builder was John Beauchamp, later to become Baron Kidderminster. He was a supporter of Richard II but these were troubled times; the king's authority was challenged and in the course of the upheavals Beauchamp and others of the king's adherents were accused of treason and executed.

*After passing Holt Castle a stile and a stream are crossed. Part way down this next field the Wychavon Way is signed off left, but continue with the Severn for about three-quarters of a mile. (The walk can actually be shortened if required by following the Wychavon Way over the wooded cliff to your left as far as the bottom of the fish ponds where you pick up the route description back to Holt Fleet, indicated later.)*

The banks of the river are tree-lined; the expected waterside lovers, willow and alders are found, but there is also oak, hazel and hawthorn, one bush acting as host to the parasitic mistletoe.

*The wood presses in closer to the river but soon falls back again. Ahead will be seen a row of houses, on a ridge sufficiently high to keep them safe from the winter floods. This is a signal that the riverside path is coming to an end. Keep with it until the field boundary is reached then cross a stile and turn left on a fenced path, soon to join the lane below the houses.*

*Turn left to follow the narrow rising lane to reach the main road, the A449, after 300 yards. The houses may keep dry enough but not so the lower part of the lane, as the flood height indicator amply demonstrates.*

*Turn left along the footpath separated from the often heavy traffic by a grassy verge which even manages to produce a wild flower or two. (A layby, passed after a short distance, makes an alternative starting point for this walk.)*

*Sinton Lodge with its wrought-iron gates bearing a large initial S, for Sandys, is passed to your left. About 350 yards beyond the lodge take the forward left fork signed to Ombersley, an attractive "black and white" village. The young king, Charles II, who was only 21 years old at the time, stopped here as he made his escape following the Royalist defeat at the battle of Worcester in 1651.*

*The route does not go fully into the village but the white-painted Crown & Sandys and the Kings Arms can be seen ahead. Three hundred yards after leaving the A449 take the path on the left signed Turn Mill. At this point we have met the Wychavon Way once more and the waymarked route is followed for a little under half a mile, as described to the western end of the pools.*

*After a few yards pass through a kissing gate and forward over the field to a stile at the corner of the wood seen ahead. Follow the outside edge of the wood to the top end of the field as it skirts Black Pool. At the top of the field go through a wide gap in the hedge and carry on with the fish pools to your left but screened at first by thick woodland; when they eventually appear they prove to be further camouflaged by a thick bed of reeds.*

Away to your right will be seen Ombersley Court in its parkland setting. The house, circa 1725, was built as the residence of the first Lord Sandys. When we passed this way last the field was sown with flax, its flower heads spreading a pale blue haze up the slope. Flax is grown for both cattle food and for linseed oil, the taller variety's longer fibres being used for linen. A pleasant change from the more aggressive luminescent yellow flowering of the now more common oil seed rape.

*Part way down the field edge the path is signed off forward left to follow the large tree-shaded fish pond and the occasional plop of a fish leaping for a fly. The Wychavon Way is left at the foot of the pond where the path meets a wide track.*

The Turn Mill promised by the footpath sign has long gone, although a deep cut in the dam retaining wall marks the place where the wheel once turned powered by the large head of water held in the extensive ponds.

*From the bottom of the pond turn right, ie. northwards, taking the wide track through trees which runs in a hollow way with hedges spilling over the exposed layers of sandstone.*

*After a short distance the track comes into the open and a path is signed off to the left; ignore this unless you wish to return by the river bank. Three hundred yards after leaving the pool take the path on the left (found by an electricity sub-station) which heads north-west over the fields towards Power's Farm. The more open aspect now provides some distant views. Retrospectively, half left to the summits of the Malvern Hills, you can see the spire of Hallow's church, and through the trees the great central tower of Worcester cathedral and the high-rise flats on the opposite side of the river at St Johns. Forward there is a fine prospect of the semi-circular profile of the Abberley, Walgrove and Woodbury Hills with the clock tower clearly outlined between the first two (explored in the next walk).*

At the end of the track bear right, passing Randal's House to reach a lane where you turn left. Shortly after passing Power's Farm turn left (by the brick wall), on a falling path between trees, soon to meet and turn right on a tarmac track past houses. After about 100 yards turn left and when this track divides bear right, soon descending on a fenced path. At the foot of the short slope turn right and continue on a wide track to reach the main road. Here turn left and after 40 yards or so take the narrow lane on the right which will bring you back to the river bank and your starting point.

## 15: THE ABBERLEY HILLS

| | |
|---|---|
| *Start:* | Hundred House Hotel, Great Witley, A443 10 miles north-west of Worcester. |
| *Car Parking:* | No formal car park at start of walk. Parking at Witley Court for visitors to the church and house. |
| *Distance:* | 5½ miles. |
| *Detail:* | A three hills walk, following part of the Worcestershire Way, with fine views. |
| *Maps:* | 1:25,000 Pathfinder 973 (SO 66/76). 1:50,000 Landranger 150. |
| *Refreshments:* | Tea garden near the church at Witley Court. |

An unrelieved diet of riverside walking will sooner or later require a complete change of menu. This walk deserts the Severn entirely to make a temporary escape to the hills, albeit to viewpoints that overlook one of its major tributaries, the Teme. If time allows, this expedition may be combined with a visit to Witley Court and church, one of the show pieces of the county.

Witley Court, now in the caring hands of English Heritage, is signed off from the A443 about a mile east of Great Witley. The original house has been the subject of "home extensions" on the grand scale with the fountains in the gardens reflecting the splendour of the mansion.

Sadly, disaster struck in 1937 when the house was damaged by fire and alas was never restored. The roofless shell has been made safe and various areas are gradually being reopened and there are ambitious plans by the Poseidon Society to put the magnificent

*Witley Court, Great Witley*

fountains in full working order. Nevertheless, the house is never likely to be restored to its former glory except perhaps in the mind's eye of the increasing number of visitors which it attracts.

No such effort of imagination is required to appreciate the adjacent church of St Michael and All Angels built by Lord Foley, one of the former owners of the court. There can be few first time visitors who do not give a gasp of surprise when they pass through the great door, for here is what has been described as one of the finest baroque churches in England, its interior decoration a symphony in gold and white. The modest coin required to illuminate the finely painted ceiling of Antonio Bellucci is amply repaid. No less rewarding are the painted windows, as bright as the day Joshua Price laid down his brush nearly 200 years ago, whilst the memorial to its builder is monumental in every sense of the word.

## THE WALK

*The walk starts on the west side of the Hundred House Hotel, a former coaching inn, on a signed path which runs alongside the inn. After a short distance this swings to the right for a few yards then continues uphill, following the line of the hedge on your right and heading towards the woods. A backward glance produces a view over pleasant rolling country. In the distance will be seen the long whale-back shape of Bredon Hill, behind which runs the main scarp of the Cotswolds.*

*At the top of the field cross a stile and take a further look back to the outline of the northern end of the Malvern Hills before continuing to the woods. Here the path climbs steeply through broadleaved woodland. After about 100 yards a T-junction of paths is met; turn right, losing height but soon climbing again and gradually swinging to the right.*

*After a while the path bears to the left and is joined by a distinct path coming in from the right. Turn left to follow the ridge north-westerly with the slopes to your right falling sharply away and occasional glimpses of the landscape below. As the triangulation point (928ft) is approached the trees to your left recede to give long views, with Abberley Hall and its famous clock tower attracting attention.* During the campaign of Owen Glendower's rebellion it is said that Henry IV's troops took up a position on the hill with aggressive intentions toward the forces of the Welsh who had secured themselves within the old fort on Woodbury Hill. There is, however, no great battle of Witley to report; light skirmishing to test out each other's strength left neither side prepared to commit their men to full-scale hostilities.

*Continue from the triangulation point, soon dropping downhill to meet a broad crossing path; turn right with this descending to meet the lane from Abberley village. Turn left along the lane, continuing with the Worcestershire Way, a 39 mile regional route between Kingsford Country Park in the north of the county to Malvern.* (A full guide to the route is published by Hereford and Worcester County Council and should be available from bookshops and Tourist Information Offices, or direct from County Hall, Spetchly Road, Worcester WR5 2NP.)

*Follow the usually quiet and pleasant lane for about 600 yards to the main road, the A443. Take the path immediately opposite, signed public bridleway Standford Road, a broad track which is followed for just over half a mile.*

The way, lined with beech, Scots pine and oak, provides views

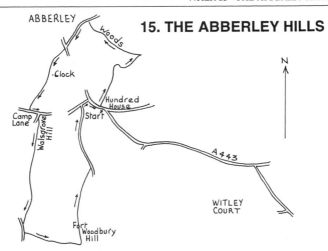

## 15. THE ABBERLEY HILLS

to the Clee Hills half right - Titterstone Clee Hill may be identified by the earth satelite navigation station on its summit whilst its twin, Brown Clee Hill, the highest point in Shropshire, is similarly crowned with telecommunication technology.

Abberley Hall, which is passed on your left, is now a school, as soon becomes apparent. Overtopping the trees is a famous Worcestershire landmark, the county's answer to Big Ben, a quite magnificent clock tower with its four faces proclaiming the time of the day quite accurately. The Hall dates from the mid-nineteenth century, with the tower, regarded by some as a folly, erected in 1883 by John Jones, the son of the house, as a memorial tribute to his father.

*Continue along the bridleway and after passing through wrought-iron gates turn left on the B4203 which is followed for 200 yards as far as Turnpike Cottage. Here turn right to follow Camp Lane, and after about 100 yards take the path signed on the left - still on the Worcestershire Way.*

*The narrow but clear path climbs half right to the summit ridge of Walsgrove Hill (836ft) which is followed southwards with fine views over the Teme Valley and to the Clee Hills. The ridge is followed for nearly three-quarters of a mile, crossing a succession of stiles. Shortly after entering a wood turn right on the Worcestershire Way. The path falls steeply and soon* fish-hooks left to reach Camp Lane by way of a short flight of steps.

Turn left along the lane but after a few yards take the path on the left, signed off through a gateway marked private but still on the Worcestershire Way. Go forward half right over the drive as waymarked. Soon the path climbs through a cleft in the hills to cross a stile to pass into the stygian gloom of a short stretch of pine forest to emerge into a field.

Cross the field; here the Worcestershire Way turns sharp right. Our route now leaves it so continue on to the top of the field to pass over a stile by a five-barred gate almost opposite the exit from the wood.

Go forward with the boundary of the trees to your left and with a view to the Malvern Hills forward and half right. A handsome hall is reached which commands fine views of the Teme Valley. Follow the path which runs on the outside of its garden wall towards a gate which gives on to a path following the inside edge of the wood.

After about 200 yards, after passing through a gate, with Lippett's Farm seen ahead, turn immediately left climbing the hillside towards Woodbury Camp. When the boundary fence on your right falls back, turn right with this, soon to pass a venerable sweet chestnut tree. About 50 paces from the tree turn sharp left up the bank to reach a crossing path. Go over this on a broad track heading north over the wooded summit.

Beyond the further bank of the camp maintain your direction on the descending track, ignoring the forest road which crosses your way. The path steepens; again ignore a further crossing path and continue on a narrow path which reaches a lane close to a junction with a track to Woodbury Hill Farm.

Turn left with the lane heading back towards Great Witley and the Hundred House Hotel seen prominently under the Abberley Hills. Follow the lane for half a mile, passing Walsgrove Farm on your left with its oast house and scores of pigeon holes set in the brickwork of its buildings.

The lane makes a junction with the B4203; here turn right and after 100 yards right again, and after another 200 yards return to your starting point at the Hundred House Hotel.

# 16: WORCESTER -
## the battlefields of Severn and Teme

| | |
|---|---|
| *Start:* | Worcester Racecourse, Pitchcroft, car parking just off Castle Street. |
| *Distance:* | 7 miles. |
| *Detail:* | Level walking on good paths with historical connections. |
| *Maps:* | 1:25,000 Pathfinder 996 (SO 85/95). |
| | 1:50,000 Landranger 150. |
| *Toilets:* | Riverbank near railway bridge and Bridge Street at junction with Deansway. |

*Refreshments:* Worcester including the cathedral refectory.

This walk from "The Faithful City", so named for its allegiance to the Royalist cause during the English Civil War, has echoes of the battle of September 1651. Charles II having marched south from Scotland in an attempt to regain the throne was challenged by Cromwell's Parliamentary army. Fierce fighting took place in the riverside fields to the south of Worcester, and within hours the Royalist forces were in disarray. The battle moved into the streets of the city with great loss of life, especially around the Sidbury Gate and the cathedral. As night fell the king was forced to take flight eventually to find refuge in France after one of history's great escape stories.

The story of the battle and the king's escape is told in one of Worcester's oldest secular buildings, the Commandery, located close to the cathedral near the junction of City Walls Road and Sidbury; a visit is recommended. This walk follows the Severn downstream to the city boundary, where an observation platform looks out over the battlefield and continues through the fields in which part of the battle took place.

## THE WALK

Racing has taken place at Pitchcroft for over 350 years and it was here that the Royalist cavalry was assembled in 1651. The racecourse lies close to the river; winter flooding may leave the course and the car park under several feet of water.

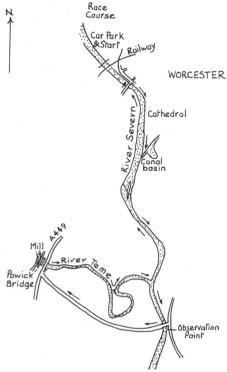

N

Race
Course

Car Park
& Start

Railway

WORCESTER

Cathedral

River Severn

Canal
basin

A449

Mill

River Teme

Powick
Bridge

Observation
Point

## 16. WORCESTER, SEVERN AND TEME

*From the car park turn right along Croft Road, passing the Severn View Hotel. This was the point at which earlier bridges gave access to the city until 1781 when the present five-arched sandstone bridge was built a little to the south.*

*Cross Bridge Street, but not the bridge, to continue downstream, passing the former warehouses which now have a new lease of life following conversion to flats and a restaurant. The tall spire to your left is all that remains of St Andrew's Church; its elegant lines have earned it the soubriquet The Glover's Needle, doubly apt since the city was once*

the centre of a major glove-making industry.

The road narrows to become a riverside walk which passes the cathedral watergate where markers indicate the heights of successive floods from the seventeenth century. November 1770 holds the record but only just, for the great flood of December 1947 was only a fraction short of the mark.

Walkers who have set a full day aside for this expedition may have time for an early diversion to visit the cathedral. Its history is a long one, with successive churches built on the site since the seventh century. King John was buried here between two of its bishops at his special request and Charles II climbed the tower to watch the progress of the battle that was to send him back into exile until the restoration of the monarchy in 1660. Sir Edward Elgar, the musical darling of his day, had a long association with the cathedral, which is one of the revolving venues of the Three Choirs Festival.

*The riverside path continues to Diglis where the Worcester and Birmingham Canal makes its junction with the Severn.* Birmingham is 30 miles, 58 locks and 5 tunnels away. In contrast the construction of the 42 mile Severn Navigation between Gloucester and Stourport required only 6 locks to maintain the levels for its busy commercial deep-water operations, with only one lock to be negotiated from this point in the 16 miles to Tewkesbury.

*The promised lock is soon reached, the twin Diglis Locks with the path continuing for a further mile to the new bridge which crosses the river at the city boundary. Just beyond the bridge take the path which climbs to the battlefield observation point. Here a series of descriptive panels show the scene as it was on the afternoon of 3 September 1651.*

The view is not only of the battlefield but a wider prospect which includes the Woodbury and Abberley Hills, Clee Hills in Shropshire and closer at hand the 9 mile run of the Malvern Hills culminating in the 1394ft-high Worcestershire Beacon.

*From the viewpoint cross the road and follow the bypass over the Severn. Field paths may be joined later but the roadside path can be conveniently followed to the roundabout, then bear right towards Worcester and the River Teme. After a short distance take the footpath on the right and turn immediately left under the bridge. Cross the short field to climb to the old road which crosses the Teme by Powick Bridge.*

The bridge had a part to play in two of the Civil War actions. During the battle of Worcester in 1651 it was breached by the defenders in order to protect the approaches to the city. Fierce fighting took place in this area with the Royalist troops coming under attack after a crossing of the Severn and Teme had been made by Cromwell's troops using boat bridges. One of the earliest engagements of the Civil War also took place near here when Royalist cavalry under the command of Prince Rupert defeated a small Parliamentarian force in pursuit of a waggon train carrying a consignment of silver from Oxford to bolster the King's war chest.

*Once over the bridge turn right and follow the Temeside path*

*Powick Bridge and the River Teme*

downstream for half a mile. The path then swings to the left, leaving the river, but soon rejoins it and continues to meet the Severn. Follow the Severn upstream for three-quarters of a mile to the weir, a favourite spot for hopeful fishermen casting their lines in pursuit of salmon.

From the weir continue upstream with an opportunity for photographers to capture the famous view of the cathedral from the riverside. The Worcestershire County Cricket Club ground lies back a little on your left but it too is subject to flooding when the river is in full spate. Cross the bridge and turn left along Croft road to return to your starting point.

## 17: OLD HILLS and MADRESFIELD

*Start:*      Old Hills, located on the B4424 (western side of River Severn, 5 miles north of Upton upon Severn and 4 miles south of Worcester via the A449 and B4424 from Powick.

*Car Parking:*    Small car park on edge of Old Hills just beyond bend in the road.

| | |
|---|---|
| *Detail:* | Field, woodland and riverside paths explore a very gently rolling landscape with fine views. Mostly level walking, one short steep climb. Winter flooding can leave the riverside path from Rhydd and the lower meadows to the east of Frieze Wood under water. |
| *Distance:* | 8 miles approx. |
| *Maps:* | 1:25,000 Pathfinder 1019 (SO 84/94). |
| | 1:50,000 Landranger 150. |

This walk includes several attractive features, not the least a quite remarkable dovecote on the Madresfield estate, but let the story unfold as the walk progresses. It should be noted that recent waymarking indicates some minor changes to rights of way so the textual description may not exactly match your copy of the map. While the route is fairly easy to follow some muddy sections, but not outrageously so, will be encountered and boots are recommended.

Despite the presence of the small car park walkers arriving at Old Hills will immediately encounter an almost timeless rural scene as a gaggle of geese and a scatter of hens patrol the common near the road with sheep grazing the hillside.

## THE WALK

*From the car park join the track which runs westward past the row of attractive cottages which edge the common, one with a witch and broomstick weather vane. The track gives way to grass as the cottages are left behind but maintain your direction with a gentle climb to the triangulation point.*

To your right is a brief and distant glimpse of the sandstone central tower of Worcester Cathedral and the slender white spire of St Andrew's Church, locally called The Glover's Needle - a commemoration of the gloving industry that once flourished in the city.

*From the triangulation point make a short easy descent by the wide grassy path ignoring the several tracks which cross your way.*

The partial view to the Malvern Hills, which will be in sight for much of this walk, includes its highest point, the Worcestershire Beacon, 1394ft, and North Hill. Sir Edward Elgar, believed by many to be the greatest English composer for 200 years, was born at Lower Broadheath, near Worcester, and lived for many years within sight of the hills from which it is said he found the inspiration for some of his works.

*At the foot of the short slope go forward to a waymarked gate on the bridleway which heads west. In about 20 paces turn left over a stile to cross the fenced off area which contains a small pond, and over a further stile. Take the path, which passes an old oak tree leaning at a drunken angle, pursuing this diagonally over the field (south-west) to woodland seen ahead.*

*Cross a stile set about midway down the wood, New Coppice, and over a plank bridge, maintaining your direction through the wood and ignoring the crossing path. Leave the wood by a stile to join a track and turn right over a stream and beyond the gateway turn left.*

*Follow the field edge with brook to your left to reach the edge of Woodsfield Coppice. Do not enter the wood but cross the stream again,*

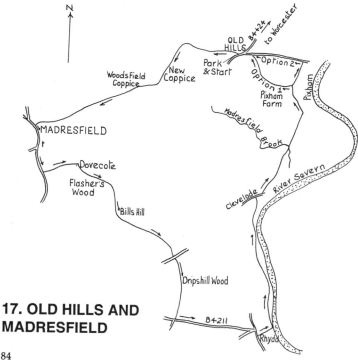

# 17. OLD HILLS AND MADRESFIELD

*passing through the gateway and turn right. Now maintain your direction, a little south of west, by waymarked field paths for three-quarters of a mile, at first with Woodsfield Coppice to your right and with the brook also a little to your right. The exits from the fields are found about 60 yards up from the right-hand field corners.*

Some tall poplars garlanded with the parasitic mistletoe will be noticed and several trees neatly drilled by woodpeckers. The full 9-mile long run of the Malvern Hills now becomes increasingly prominent, a reminder that these hills, which for centuries have marked the boundary between Herefordshire and Worcestershire, provide excellent walking and superb views.

*Leave the last field by a kissing gate and go ahead on a metalled lane which soon becomes a hollow way, passing under arched bridges which connect the grounds of Madresfield Court with some fine mature trees to be seen in the landscaped gardens.*

The grounds are occasionally open to the public with daffodil Sunday a popular event. The Court, built in the sixteenth century, can be seen, albeit distantly, later in the walk. It was for centuries the home of the Lygon family, later Earls of Beauchamp.

*After passing under a second tunnel, ignore the right fork and continue, passing a handsome house with a weather vane which bears a coronet and a large initial B, a device which will be seen several times as the walk progresses. Note also the intricate and beautifully executed brickwork of the tall chimney.*

*On reaching the road turn left with it on a footpath, passing the private drive to Madresfield Court. The Malvern Hills are again in view with the houses of Great Malvern reaching up the steep eastern slopes of the range. Honeybee Cottage is passed, dated 1869 and with the Beauchamp crest.*

Break your journey to visit Madresfield Church. The lych-gate bears the legend in red and gilt "Thou art the place to hide me in".

The attention is immediately drawn to the stone stepped and walled wellhead with a wrought-iron frame and its hoist intact. The church and graveyard has several memorials to members of the Lygon family. Readers are referred to the excellent church guide which in addition to a detailed description of the church contains brief biographies of the family and reveals the interesting dual purpose for which the well was sunk.

*From the church continue along the road for a quarter of a mile to turn* left down the driveway by the handsome lodge. Now the mellowed brick buildings of Madresfield Court and its tall spire come into view half left across the parkland.

The drive continues to Home Farm; here pause to admire the exceptionally fine dovecote, the last building on your right.

Can the humble pigeon ever have had such a handsome home? Such is the distinction of the dovecote that I am told that "people come by the coach load to view it", no doubt by prior appointment. It is a tall round brick tower with a steeply pitched tiled roof and of course the coronet and B crest. The whole, topped by a decorative weather vane which includes what appears to be the "sun in splendour", an emblem adopted by Edward IV after his success at the battle of Mortimer's Cross in 1461. Within the dovecote there are several rows of neat nesting boxes, sufficient to accommodate several hundred birds.

Immediately beyond the dovecote turn right, crossing the field with the buildings of Home Farm to your right, and make for the footpath that runs south-eastwards along the outside edge of Flasher's Wood.

When the wood falls back at a sharp angle maintain your direction to the far end of the field to pass through a gateway by a tall tree. Bear right again following the outside edge of Flasher's Wood to pass through a further metal gateway.

Continue to the opening seen ahead which leads into the wood opposite at Bills Hill. Take the broad track through the wood with the brook on your right. On leaving the wood go forward, soon to cross the stile found on your right and thence by a plank bridge over the Whiteacres Brook, and into a large field.

The way continues south-easterly towards the northern edge of South Wood. Leave the field by a former gateway, found in the hedge line about 40 yards above the wood, and follow the outside edge of the wood. As the trees fall back head diagonally over the field to meet the road, about three-quarters of a mile north-east of Guarlford.

Cross the road and take the signed path opposite which climbs to the edge of Dripshill Wood with the stile found close to the pylon.

Follow the outside edge of the wood and maintain your direction up and over the hill through four fields, keeping the fence line to your left. The Malvern Hills fill the horizon to your right.

On reaching the road (B4211) by Fowler's Farm turn left and follow *it for three-quarters of a mile to the crossroads at Rhydd. The road can be busy with fast traffic but wide grass verges should keep the walker clear of trouble. Rhydd Farm is passed on your right and the deep but dry ditch on one side of the house suggests that this may once have been the site of a moated farm.*

*On reaching the crossroads turn right, signed Upton, and once clear of the junction cross the road to take the wide track, opposite the RAC box, which falls to the River Severn.*

*Turn left to follow the signed footpath along the river bank; with no need to check the directions for the next half a mile the life of the river can be enjoyed to the full. Herons and kingfishers may be seen, ducks always, a swan or two, or a cormorant with neck outstretched taking a fast and straight flight up the river, and in summer narrowboats and cruisers. Winter walkers are however advised to take particular care along this section of the river for if the Severn has recently retreated from its annual trespass beyond its appointed boundaries the path is likely to be covered with a film of slippery silt - and the river is only a short slide away!*

*As you advance upstream the recently improved ponds to your left cover the site of a former brickfield and Brickfield Cottage will be seen beyond the ponds. The riverside path leads by way of a stile into a caravan site. When the shop is reached, by a road junction, go ahead to take the path which climbs the marl cliff seen ahead.*

*Keep the fence line and wooded cliff to your right as you continue to the top of the rise with a clump of Scots pine standing on the 150ft summit to your left.*

*The modest height provides good views over the pastures of the flood plain and the S bend of the river as it curves away from Clevelode.*

*Remain with the cliff edge as the path descends to meet and cross a stile by some horse barns. Here turn right along a closely fenced path with a steep fall to your right as you look down upon the houses of the tiny hamlet of Clevelode. Clearly these cliffs mark the line of a once broader and perhaps deeper river that is still occasionally at pains to recover lost territory.*

Once a ferry operated here transporting people and bicycles over the Severn. Downstream the nearest bridge was four miles away at Upton and until recent times five miles upstream at Worcester. Salmon was caught commercially here; the netting of the river was permitted until 1929 and in Worcester a number of families earned their living from fishing. Coal was landed at the quay and a toll house in the lane collected the appropriate charges.

*At the end of the hedged path cross a stile and turn left passing some attractive cottages to meet a lane. Here turn right, ignore the first footpath signed on the left but take the next, a wide track that climbs to Clevelode Farm with some excellent buildings no doubt constructed from local brick.*

*Pass the farm to your right and go ahead on the waymarked bridleway which rises gently over Chapel Hill and then descends towards the bottom edge of a wood to cross the Madresfield Brook. The square tower of Kempsey church will be seen in the distance.*

*Once over the bridge climb the high floodbank and descend bearing left to pass through the waymarked gateway near a pylon. Bear diagonally right over the field which is subject to winter flooding. At the corner of the field pass through a metal gateway and go ahead on a clear track with a ditch to your right.*

*The track soon curves gently to the left and as you advance the three-storied brick-built Pixham farmhouse is seen on the higher ground with a view over the meadows of the flood plain of the Severn.*

*Shortly after passing under the power lines leave the field by a metal gateway. Current maps may show a footpath heading up towards the farm but continue with the bridleway, still with the hedge on your right.* Over the fields forward right will be seen the black and white half-timbered buildings at Pixham, an ancient ferry crossing of the Severn. It is said that Henry III, captured by Simon de Montford at the battle of Lewes, 1264, during the Barons War was brought to Kempsey by the Pixham ferry.

*At the end of the field a farm lane coming in from the left is met with the bridleway continuing forward on an improved track. There are now two possible return routes:*

## Option 1

*At the junction with the farm track, pass through the waymarked blue gate and turn left following the fence line. A further waymarked gate is seen but continue up the hillside, with the ditch to your left, to meet and pass through a waymarked gate.* A backward glance as you progress up the hillside reveals the river and the whale-backed Bredon Hill, from which A.E.Houseman in his collection of poems, *A Shropshire Lad*, listened to the church bells and mourned the death of one for whom they would never ring out over the "coloured counties".

*From the gate go forward to turn right on a broad grassy track which* is followed for 100 yards to pass over a waymarked stile. The path beyond crosses a short stretch of rough ground; after a few yards turn left through a deep but dry trough, passing a thatched cottage to your left. Here a hard track is met; leave this turning right, descending to meet a lane opposite a further thatched cottage.

Turn left to follow the lane for a short distance to meet the main road opposite Ye Olde Hills Cafe. Cross the road and turn left to return to your starting point.

## Option 2

Remain with the bridleway which after 300 yards will bring you to the lane at Pixham. Here turn left, climbing steadily for nearly half a mile to reach the road opposite Ye Olde Hills Cafe. Turn left to return to your starting point.

# 18: SAXON TIMES -
# Tewkesbury to Deerhurst

| | |
|---|---|
| *Start:* | Riverside, Lower Lode Lane located on the right of the A38 south of the abbey. |
| *Car Parking &* *Picnic Site:* | At foot of lane overlooking the Severn. |
| *Distance:* | 4 miles approx. |
| *Detail:* | An easy walk on field paths over low hill to Deerhurst with a return beside the Severn. |
| *Maps:* | 1:25,000 Pathfinder 1042 (SO 83/93) and (edge of) 1066 (SO 82/92). 1:50,000 Landranger 150. |
| *Toilets:* | By car park off A38 near junction with Lower Lode Lane. |

Tewkesbury is one of our delightful small towns. Modern shops cheek by jowl with timber-framed buildings, some expertly and lovingly restored, little winding alleys and old inns from which you could believe that the stage coach has only just departed. Above all there is the quite magnificent abbey built on the grand scale which survived the dissolution to serve as the parish church.

In 1471 Tewkesbury was the site of a decisive battle in the long-running Wars of the Roses. Here the houses of York and Lancaster

*Lower Lode - ferry crossing*

fought each other in the vineyards and fields just south of the abbey; a desperate clash of arms that swept away in the blood-stained waters of the Swilgate Queen Margaret's hopes of securing the throne for her son, Edward, Prince of Wales. Edward, only 18 years old, was one of the thousands who died in the fierce fighting centred on Bloody Meadow. The Queen's loyal supporter, the Duke of Somerset, was captured and executed two days later. Margaret too was taken prisoner and held to ransom. Edward's father, the Lancastrian Henry VI, had succeeded to the throne in 1422 when he was only a year old. He was deposed in 1461, and after a brief restoration in 1470 was again imprisoned in the Tower of London. Tewkesbury sealed his fate too, murdered two weeks later as the triumphant Edward IV returned to the capital.

The story of the battle is told in the town's museum and at Bloody Meadow, which forms part of a Battlefield Trail; a leaflet is available from the Tourist Information Centre.

# 18. TEWKESBURY TO DEERHURST

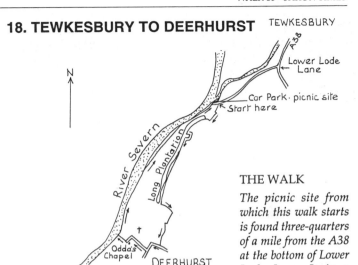

## THE WALK

*The picnic site from which this walk starts is found three-quarters of a mile from the A38 at the bottom of Lower Lode Lane. It is a* pleasant spot close to where the Avon millstream joins the Severn. The riverside is noisy with waddling mallard and strutting greylag geese not averse to feeding off the crumbs that fall from rich men's picnic tables. A ferry provides a link to the opposite bank on which stands the picturesque Lower Lode Inn, with a clutch of pleasure craft moored alongside the banks. The pleasures of the river scene must, however, be deferred as the walk takes to slightly higher ground for the outward journey.

Initially the footpaths in this area have been the subject of some sensible re-routing so that your particular edition of the map may not have caught up with the changes, but this should not present any great problem as the route has for the most part been waymarked. Incidentally, the use of "path" in this walk does not imply that it is necessarily visible as such on the ground.

*From the picnic site retrace your steps up Lower Lode Lane for 100 yards and take the path on the right-signed Deerhurst. Follow the broad track as far as the gateway to Shutman Cottage. Here turn left and immediately right, with the golf course to your left and trees and cottage to your right.*

*Continue to hug the outside edge of the trees, the Long Plantation, until*

91

you reach the end of the golf course. Turn left along the hedge with a deep hollow way to your right. After about 60 yards turn right over a stile and then immediately right. Ignore the gateway facing you which leads to the hollow way, and take the path ahead, soon to swing left again following the outside edge of the Long Plantation.

There are glimpses to the Severn through the trees but the best views are to the left where the Cotswold scarp and its outliers make the eastern horizon. Maintain your direction along the field edges and over stiles. The gateway near the coppice on Rayer's Hill gives a good forward view to the distant Cotswolds, which look particularly fine when the morning light of a late autumn day breaks through the clouds to provide a nicely atmospheric silhouette of the hills.

As you near the end of the Long Plantation the path descends; ignore the gate on the right and swing left, soon to pass a pond on your right. A little beyond the pond take the stile on your right and turn right along the hedge, passing the pond and then bearing left up the field edge.

About 60 yards on from the pond cross a footbridge almost hidden in the hedge and turn left on the raised bank at the field edge. Over the meadow to your right a farm and then Deerhurst church come into view. Continue with the hedge line, crossing further stiles to reach a lane.

Turn right with the lane and keep with it as it curves past the entrance to Priory Farm and in 100 yards turn right signed to Deerhurst Church and Odda's Chapel. There is a good view to the church through the willow trees; a visit should not be neglected for it is full of interest.

The Priory Church of St Mary originated in a celtic foundation; the present church dates from 700 AD and is valued as an outstanding Anglo-Saxon building. Towards the end of the tenth century the young Alphege came here as a novice monk. From this quiet corner of Gloucestershire the saintly man moved on to become Abbot of Bath, and later when Archbishop of Canterbury to meet a martyr's death at the hands of the Danes after he had been held to ransom - a ransom which he bravely instructed should not be paid. Among the church's treasures is the splendid tomb of Sir John Cassy, Chief Baron of the Exchequer and dead these 600 years. Set in the ancient stained-glass window is the victorious Edward IV's symbol of the sun in splendour, beneath which is the martyred Catherine with her wheel and the faithful Alphege.

Return to the lane which passes through the gap with its slots for *floodgates and by the tall marker which demonstrates the great depth of the Severn when in full flood.*

The late Saxon building, Odda's Chapel, now in the care of English Heritage, is soon met on your left. A remarkable place, no less so for its having been "lost" for centuries. It was built ten years before the Norman Conquest by Odda in memory of his brother Elfric. Inside is a replica of the foundation stone found in a nearby field in 1675, but it was two centuries later that the chapel itself was rediscovered. It had in fact been there all the time, staring everyone in the face, but following a secular career as part of the adjoining timber-framed farm.

*From the chapel return to the lane and turn left. After a few yards bear right through a metal gateway and go ahead to reach the Severn. Turn right to follow this pleasant stretch of the river upstream for a mile and a half to return to your starting point. The last few yards pass the boathouse of the Cheltenham Ladies College, on which is noted the highwater mark of the notorious floods of 1947.*

## 19: HAW BRIDGE AND SANDHURST HILL, with shortened route from Sandhurst village

| | |
|---|---|
| *Start:* | Haw Bridge on the B4213, 3 miles west of the A38 and 3 miles south of Tewkesbury. |
| *Distance:* | 7¼ miles. Alternative start from Sandhurst 5 mile circuit - see end of text for detail. |
| *Detail:* | Pleasant riverside walking following the east bank downstream to the Red Lion then over the cliff to continue along the riverside, returning via the modest height of Sandhurst Hill and the Red Lion (again!). Some paths may be very wet in winter. It should be remembered that the Severn when in flood may rise rapidly and the meadows are sometimes under water. |
| *Maps:* | 1:25,000 Pathfinder 1066 (SO 82/92). 1:50,000 Landranger 162. |
| *Refreshments:* | The Red Lion, Wainlode. |

The Haw Bridge we see today is a modern construction dating from 1961 but situated on the site of a centuries-old ferry. The river was first bridged in 1824 at the behest of the enterprising businessmen of Cheltenham with an eye to increasing the town's trade with South-West Wales by diverting traffic from its rival, Gloucester. A plaque on the bridge describes it as "... a graceful three span structure with slender cast iron ribs ...". It was clearly an asset to the river scene whether or not it succeeded in the intention to milch some of Gloucester's trade. It served the traveller well for 124 years until disaster struck. Nemesis unkindly came in the guise of a large ship riding the winter floods of 1958 and hitting the bridge, which was so badly damaged that rebuilding was the only option.

The once busy commercial activity of the river and its important crossings is perhaps demonstrated by the number of inns along its banks. Half a mile upstream is the Coal House Inn at Apperley with a sign which reinforces the origins of its name: one of Fluck and Rowbottam's narrowboats making a delivery. The western side of Haw Bridge has two inns, the New Inn, and one named after the bridge with a sign which depicts two river activities, a fisherman in a punt quietly dozing over his rod with the old bridge in the background, and the reverse of the sign bringing matters up to date with a holiday cruiser passing under the modern bridge.

A mile downstream is a further inn, The Red Lion, and after two miles on the opposite bank the Boat Inn marks another ferry crossing at Ashleworth Quay.

## THE WALK

*From the eastern bank of the Severn take the path which descends to a wicket gate and past Bridge House to leave by a stile to join the riverside path.* Pollarded willows line the bank: the two inns and the bridge add their reflections in the water to those of the boats moored at the landing stage. In spring, house martins swoop down to the water's edge collecting mud to build their nests.

The Severnside meadows south of Tewkesbury provide grazing for fine cattle, black and white fresians and the distinct brown and white Herefords, a native breed that spread round the world.

*As Haw Farm, on the opposite bank, is approached, the river is left for a while as the path bears left over a stile then immediately right to follow* the hedge line. *The path continues following the floodbank through the meadows with the cliff at Wainlode coming into view.*

*A mile downstream from Haw Bridge the now disused Coombe Hill Canal is crossed, a two and a half mile cut through the meadows to The Wharf to take riverborne coal a little closer to Cheltenham.*

*Continue on the floodbank, passing some venerable oaks.* In season the meadowland attracts butterflies and dragonflies and the

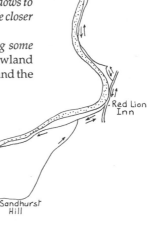

## 19. HAW BRIDGE AND SANDHURST HILL

walker may send a partridge skyward in sudden alarm, a ground-hugging bird that would almost certainly have been passed unnoticed had it remained still.

*A deep but unimpressive ditch is crossed and here a stile bears a notice with the legend NO ELVERING.* For those unfamiliar with the river some explanation may be required. Each spring the last stage of a still mysterious migration occurs in our rivers, particularly those of the south-west such as the Severn and Wye. Eels spawn in the Sargasso Sea in the Caribbean, the larvae are carried on the warm ocean currents to the seas around Europe, and as thin, finger length elvers make their way upstream to grow to maturity.

Uncountable millions of these tiny creatures flood up the River Severn in late March and early April, a brief but busy catching season. Simple equipment brings in the harvest: large handheld nets, a bucket and a bright light. As dusk falls the riverside is aglow with the dancing lights as the elvers are landed, scooped up in great numbers. The word is that the elvers, like oysters, have a powerful aphrodisiac effect; that may be so but a great deal of the catch goes for export to stock European rivers and lakes.

*The River Chelt is next encountered, where you turn right to follow the road to the Red Lion with its golden cockerel weather vane.* Within, glass cases display the monster catches of past years, bearing out the truth of at least some fishermen's tales of ones that didn't get away. There is a collection of rudd caught in 1901 and a 4lb 14oz trout caught on a dusty miller in the same year.

**\*\*(Walkers following the shortened circuit from Sandhurst should now join the cliff and riverside route southwards as follows, and on climbing the lane back to Brawn Farm turn right to return to the village.)**

*Beyond the inn the land on the east side of the river rises quickly with the river curving under The Cliff, a two-toned face in red and limey hues which disappears as vegetation clothes the less steep areas.*

*From the Red Lion leave the road to take the path forward right, crossing a stile by a Severn Way sign and climbing steadily. A backward glance reveals the long line of the Malvern Hills in the north-west. A further stile is crossed to follow the field boundary with the hedge to your right. In summer the call of a curlew may be heard from the fields beyond the river. At the end of the field cross a stile and in a few paces turn right over a further stile to follow the path through the wood. Beyond the wood the path follows the hillside with the river out of sight, a narrow and sometimes overgrown tread with teasles along the way. A steep descent through trees is eased by steps.*

*When the path emerges into the open and beyond a stile, turn half right to follow the floodbank for a mile to reach the lane opposite Ashleworth Quay. The Boat Inn and the spire of the church can be seen across the water and are included in the next walk.*

*Cross the stile into the lane and turn left to follow it for just over half a mile to Brawn Farm.*

*The lane climbs steadily first between willow and ash, later in a bramble-covered hawthorn-hedged hollow way.*

*An old orchard with now unfashionably tall trees is passed as you reach Brawn Farm, with a handsome white house to your right and the semi-derelict buildings to your left destined, it seems, for a new lease of life as*

Lower Astley Wood
The Severn from Wainlode Hill

*barn conversions.*

*Beyond the white house the track divides, the right fork to Sandhurst village, but turn left through a waymarked gateway/stile.*

*\* (Walkers starting from Sandhurst join the route here.)*

*Follow the broad track climbing gently to reach the triangulation point on Sandhurst Hill in three-quarters of a mile.*

Twin ponds are passed just beyond the farm, an important feature of a hill-top farm when horses and cattle needed to be watered; now the ubiquitous mallard has found a home on the willow-fringed waters. As you climb pause to look at the rooftops of Gloucester and the cathedral tower. To your left lies the riverside village of Ashleworth with its short spire topping the church tower. The Malvern Hills are again seen in the distance, looking particularly attractive when snow covered on a bright winter's day.

The widening view includes the Severn, more prominent when carrying the heavy burden of winter rain with the sun highlighting the white-painted span of Haw Bridge. A southward glance will reveal May Hill near Newent. If like the Malverns it has a dusting of snow it resembles a seasonal Christmas pudding with the distinctive clump of trees on its summit doing duty as the traditional holly sprig. The bank that cuts off the view to the right gives way to a low hedge to return the view to the Cotswolds, and closer at hand the flooded meadows act like a giant mirror, sparkling in the winter sunshine against the dark background of the hills. Forward right a tall tower block identifies the spa town of Cheltenham.

The modest height of Sandhurst Hill, 282ft, provides an excellent prospect of the green Gloucestershire countryside with its pastures, wooded hedgerows and plantations.

*Just beyond the triangulation point the path divides; ignore the half right fork and continue towards the Dutch barn seen ahead in front of a block of woodland. On reaching the barn pass it on your left and maintain your direction, keeping on the bridleway on the outside edge of the wood.*

*As you leave the summit plateau there is another fine view to the Cotswolds, the whale-backed Bredon Hill and other Cotswold outliers. Maintain your direction with Haw Bridge coming into view again and the Malvern Hills more prominent. The scene opens up to include Cleeve*

*Worcester cathedral from the river*

Common with its radio masts, the highest point of the Cotswolds.

The way continues down a gentle slope to pass through a gateway/stile at the bottom of the field. Continue, with the wood on your left.

At the foot of the hill turn right over a stile and with a hedge to your left descend to the riverside and the Red Lion, whence your steps may be retraced to your starting point at Haw Bridge.

## SHORTENED ROUTE FROM SANDHURST VILLAGE. 5 miles approx.

Sandhurst village is reached from the A38 by narrow winding lanes. A generously sized car park is located by the church.

From the car park turn right to follow the lane northwards. When the lane divides ignore the left fork signed Mussel End and continue, signed Rodway Lane. The quiet rising lane soon offers views to the Cotswolds on your right and back to the rooftops of Gloucester.

Brawn Farm is reached in three-quarters of a mile; here continue forward through a waymarked gate/stile, passing the farm to your left and now following the detailed description marked * in the foregoing text, which will take you to the Red Lion. The return by the cliff and riverside path, signed Severn Way, just south of the Red Lion is described in the main text at point **. On reaching the top of Brawn Lane turn right to return to Sandhurst, following the lane as in your outward journey.


# 20: HAW BRIDGE AND ASHLEWORTH

| | |
|---|---|
| *Start:* | Haw Bridge on the B4213, 3 miles west of the A38, 3 miles south of Tewkesbury. |
| *Distance:* | 6 miles. |
| *Detail:* | Out by the riverside to Ashleworth with its 500 year old tithe barn, returning by field paths and lanes. Winter walkers should note that the low-lying meadows are subject to flooding, as are the lanes between Tirley and Ashleworth. |
| *Maps:* | 1:25,000 Pathfinder 1066 (SO 82/92).<br>1:50,000 Landranger 162. |
| *Refreshments:* | Two inns at Haw Bridge and Boat Inn at Ashleworth. |

*The Severn at Haw Bridge*

This walk starts on the west bank of the river which is followed downstream for three miles to the small village of Ashleworth. The old towpath, dating from the early eighteenth century, kept to this side of the river from Upton upon Severn, but transferred to the opposite bank at Ashleworth. The proprietors of the towpath, which was designed for horses rather than the two-legged bow hauliers, extracted a toll for the use of the path. There were moorings at Haw Bridge with coal being delivered by barge and taking a return cargo of hay. Today much of the river bank is edged with trees and bushes; nature reclaiming territory lost when the towing path was constructed.

## THE WALK

*Head downstream, passing the Haw Bridge Inn and moorings and through a neatly constructed V nick in a gate. Continue on the broad track, passing an architectural mix of houses to your right:* a brick-built house dated

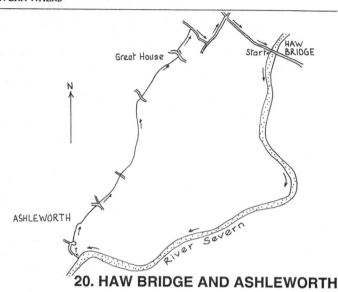

## 20. HAW BRIDGE AND ASHLEWORTH

1868, two or three neat timber-framed cottages and a house of great character, at first sight of more modern appearance but which I am told has its origins in a smaller sixteenth-century cottage. Attracting particular notice is a long brick building, now a private residence, which operated as a Malt House. Its size suggests that if this was its sole purpose it must have drawn its barley from a wider area than the immediate locality; it was of course ideally situated.

*The riverside is followed to Ashleworth via a succession of stiles with the water levels of the low-lying fields, Hasfield Ham, Ashleworth Ham and Ashleworth Meadows controlled by a network of streams and deep ditches and sluice gates as they reach the Severn.* Although the normal tidal limit of the river is indicated on the map at Maisemore Bridge on the west channel further downstream, winter walkers in particular may note that there is a tidal influence.

*As progress is made the rather more substantial sluice gates that control the exit to the river of the Coombe Hill Canal and the River Chelt will be observed on the opposite bank as the Red Lion, also out of reach, comes into view.*

*Beyond the inn the river curves under a high cliff of muted colours,* muddy red, limey, a slaty blue/grey and a thin strata leaking a red rust that suggests a small vein of iron ore may be present.

At last the spire of Ashleworth church comes into view and shortly after passing under the power lines, the edge of the village is heralded by the Boat Inn. Its inn sign proclaims a greater maritime activity than the collection of fishing punts gathered at the quayside, for the artist has portrayed a ship in full sail on deep waters set against a pale blue sky.

Below Ashleworth lies the Long Reach and in two and a quarter miles the river divides at Upper Parting to be reunited below Gloucester, but our route now deserts the river.

*Turn right up the lane, passing through the floodgates, beyond which lies a pond noisy with geese and ducks, soon to reach the tithe barn, now in the care of the National Trust.* The stone barn was built in generous proportions in anticipation of a bountiful harvest. It is about 125ft long, with twin entrances from the lane each with eaves-tall double oak iron-studded doors for easy access by wagons. Inside, great baulks of timber hold the framework that supports the heavy stone-tiled roof. The barn is still in use but is open for inspection during the summer months.

*Continue along the lane for a short distance, with the church to your right; it is worth a visit for it has some interesting features.* Like the village, it suffers from the Severn's yearly incursions and inside has the floodmark of 1947, indicating a level of water about 4ft above the pews. There is scarcely a riverside village or town that did not mark the date and it is still the measure by which subsequent floods are judged.

*As a bend in the lane is reached, take the signed footpath, passing the new burial ground on your left, and follow the hedgerow with its line of tall poplars.* There is a view to the wooded hills beyond the Severn and more distantly to the long hump back of Bredon Hill.

*Ignore the first stile seen on the left and the broad stile set at the top of the field. Here bear right along the field edge and then left, still following the hedge line.* Over the field lies the impressive timber-framed building of Ashleworth Manor House, older by 40 years than the tithe barn.

*Remain with the field edge after passing a pond and at the top corner cross a stile, going forward to meet the road by a T-junction.* I have to relate a slightly curious incident here. Walking through these fields in late January I found the stile completely blocked by part of a huge willow tree. The sawn trunk, like a great cheese, was fully 4ft high and so heavy that it was quite impossible to manhandle, but it had been brought here by the flood that had only just receded from the road. The full depth of the inundation was amply demonstrated by the straw debris deposited on the hedge tops.

About three-quarters of a mile along the lane to Tirley roadside hides of the Gloucester Trust for Nature Conservation allow a discreet view over the flooded meadows of Ashleworth Ham. Access to the reserve is by permit only but the hides give an excellent view of the hundreds of ducks that find a winter home here. Whooper swans will also be seen - and heard! The slightly higher ground of our return route gives a view over the ham. If you happen to be there when a group of swans take off you will be in no doubt of the enormous power of their great whirring flight.

*From the lane, cross to the signed path; most of the return is waymarked with the field paths heading generally north-easterly. Go directly ahead and at the end of the third field cross a stile, a crossing path and plank bridge. Now bear half right to meet a V-shaped stile and cross a stream. Now make for the diagonally opposite corner of the field with the exit found a little to the left of a group of three trees. Go forward with the hedge to your right to leave by a waymarked gate close to Colway's Farm and found 60 yards beyond the first exit from the field.*

There is now an excellent view over the reserve's extensive flood meadows. *Turn left, passing a long barn, to cross a farm track. If you think that the double gates topped with barbed wire seem unfriendly there is good reason for it; beyond lies a deep slurry pit. Continue with the fence to your left and at the far end of the field cross a stile and turn right, passing through a gateway with Villa Farm coming into view ahead. Forward half left is Hasfield Court, a fine picture of an English country house, resting content in its environment.*

*Soon a lane is met and crossed, with the way continuing through an orchard beyond a wicket gate. Cross the next field, leaving by a gateway whose waymark has been overgrown by brambles. Great House is seen ahead, built in brick, stone and timber. Bear diagonally right towards the marker post, then over a short field to a stile to meet Great House Lane. Cross the lane to the signed path, keeping to the hedgerow. At the end of the field the territory looks at first glance to be distinctly private. Cross the bridge over a ditch and head through an orchard and garden to meet a lane;*

*any doubts you may be having will be resolved by a footpath sign pointing back the way you have come.*

*Turn right to follow the lane for 300 yards to a T-junction. Turn left and when you meet a further junction turn right to return to Haw Bridge.*

# 21: FRAMPTON ON SEVERN

| | |
|---|---|
| *Start:* | Splatt Bridge, Church End, Frampton on Severn. Car park on east side of the Gloucester and Sharpness Canal. |
| *Distance:* | 3 miles approx. |
| *Detail:* | Level walking on good paths throughout. |
| *Maps:* | 1:25,000 Pathfinder 1112 (SO 70). 1:50,000 Landranger 162. |
| *Refreshments:* | Frampton on Severn. |

Frampton on Severn must count as one of the best of the Severnside villages with a great air of spaciousness afforded to it by the huge village green, one of the largest in England. The rich variety of the buildings which lie on both sides of the green is reason enough for the inclusion of this short walk. Three ponds, with attendant swans, thatched cottages, an ancient barn, the splendid orangery of Frampton Court, beflowered inns and much more provide many opportunities for the photographer in search of architectural styles or the unashamedly picturesque. He may even capture on film a strutting peacock displaying his feathered glories and for once even the majestic swan appears less regal before this great Shah.

THE WALK

*From the car park go forward to cross the swing bridge over the Gloucester and Sharpness Canal, a wide deep-water channel completed in 1827.* The canal greatly eased the considerable hazards of navigation in the lower Severn, allowing quite large sea-going ships to proceed upriver to give a great boost to the trade of the city and port of Gloucester. An inspired touch of dignity is given to the waterway by the mini doric-columned entrances to the bridgekeeper's cottages.

From the bridge look across the low-lying fields to the greater expanse of the Severn with its sand banks that at low water occupy

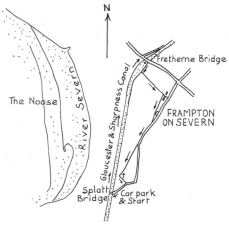

more space than the river itself. At this point the river, having completed its great horseshoe loop (described and viewed from the heights of the Forest of Dean in the Newnham walk), has broadened to nearly one and a half miles with the exposed muddy beige of the Noose accounting for all but 300 yards. Add the swift running tide and shifting sands and the need for the canal could scarcely be better demonstrated.

## 21. FRAMPTON ON SEVERN

From Splatt Bridge Frampton's church sitting almost alone in the fields looks its best, especially attractive when banks of white cloud pile up behind its sunlit tower.

*The towpath is followed northwards for just over a mile to Fretherne Bridge.* Entertainment is provided by small convoys of cruisers, more colourful narrowboats and perhaps a long line of competitive and ever hopeful anglers. Away to your left rising above the Severn is the high ground of the Royal Forest of Dean, the regal addition dating from the Norman kings when it became their exclusive hunting preserve.

*On reaching the bridge cross the canal and turn right along the bank. After about 100 yards cross a stile and turn left on the path which edges a deep drainage ditch, its opposite bank hung with a great abundance of fruit, out-of-reach blackberries and elderberry bowed down with huge clusters of shotgun-like pellets and purpled fruit. Lapwings fly low over the fields to your right, in summer perhaps only in ones and twos in contrast to the great flocks that crowd the fields in winter.*

*At the end of the field cross the small plank bridge and after a few steps go over a further stile to head along the field edge to the stile seen ahead. The path now edges one of the long barns of Manor Farm before emerging into*

*Frampton Church from the Gloucester and Sharpness Canal*

*Frampton by the village green. Turn right to head back to the starting point, but first a little exploration would not be out of order. The path to the left leads past a house with an attractive gable end dovecote. Further on, the brick frontage of the Bell Inn which overlooks the cricket pitch is relieved by an ambitious collection of hanging baskets.*

On the eastern side of the green is the Orangery and behind its high wall Frampton Court, built in 1731. Opposite and older by far is the Manor House, home for generations of Cliffords. There is a nicely romantic association, for it was here that Jane Clifford was born, Henry II's "Fair Rosamund", and later as a young woman she met the future king of England by the riverside - thus one of the great legendary romances of history began.

*At the southern end of the green, after passing the Three Horseshoes, continue along the village road, here known as The Street, which is soon left to pass through the restored lych-gate seen on your right.* The house close by the gate has an odd weather vane for one so close to God's acre: a witch on a broomstick counterbalanced by her familiar black cat.

*From the lych-gate follow the track which heads through a handsome avenue of chestnut trees to the church.* The view to the right is curtailed by the high bank of the canal and it is a strange sight to see a shiny white cruiser apparently riding waterless and ghost-like over the fields.

*After visiting the church, turn left down the lane and after a short distance right, pass Tanhouse Farm to return to your starting point.*

# 22: THE ARLINGHAM HORSESHOE

| | |
|---|---|
| *Start:* | Old Passage Inn, Arlingham, east bank of river. Leave the A38 about 8 miles south-west of Gloucester, taking the B4071 signed Frampton and continue to cross the Glouces- ter and Sharpness canal. From Arlingham village continue with the road signed Arlingham Passage. |
| *Distance:* | 6 miles approx. |
| *Detail:* | Level walking on good grassy paths and lanes with excellent views of the river and its wildlife. Boots are recommended, for the paths although mostly mud-free can be very wet from heavy dew or recent rain. Glorious as it can be in summer, the floodbanks are very exposed and the sharp winds that sometimes blow up the river may require an extra layer of clothing. |
| *Maps:* | 1:25,000 Pathfinder 1088 (SO 61/71). NB: does not totally cover route with a minute section of 1112 required for completeness, but not strictly necessary if not already in your map library. <br> 1:50,000 Landranger 162. |
| *Refreshments:* | Old Passage Inn, or in Arlingham village. |

Between Framilode and Fretherne the Severn makes a huge serpentine diversion, covering eight miles instead of the single mile needed for a more direct route. Arlingham, a small but attractive village, is situated in the centre of this loop. North, south and west of the village the land is low lying, not a contour line to be seen on the map, and the occasional spot height fails to reach double figures. Evidence of the regular incursions of the river in the past is to be found in the almost total absence of buildings; but the danger has been reduced by improvements to the floodbank and deepening of the ditches which help drain the land.

Exceptions to the "no buildings rule" is a group of barns and more notably the Old Passage Inn from which this walk starts. The inn is reached from Arlingham village by the untypically straight Passage Road. Lying just below the floodbank, the inn served the needs of travellers using the ferry that operated between here and Newnham for hundreds of years.

*Newnham from the centre of the Arlingham Horseshoe*

The major part of the walk follows the floodbank, its modest height providing wide views of the river and the surrounding landscape. Much of the land is given over to pasture, cattle in the fields, sheep on the floodbank, but most interest is likely to centre on the birdlife of the area. In late September, when the route was walked for this book, flocks of lapwings and rooks whirled over the newly ploughed fields; gulls, those ubiquitous survivors who find a living in all sorts of terrain, shrieked over both the river and land; and a little aerial armada of ducks winged its way upstream. Groups of waders and gulls paddled along the sand banks, dunlins and lapwings dwarfed by the herons which are to be found here throughout the year. No fewer than five of these magnificent birds took off from one pool at our approach. Amidst the hurly-burly of the whirring lapwings and gulls, larks rose singing on the wind despite their reputation for quietness in the late summer. The sand banks and wetlands of the Severn are famous for wintering wildfowl and as the season advances greater numbers of birds may be expected (they don't all go to the Wildfowl Trust at Slimbridge).

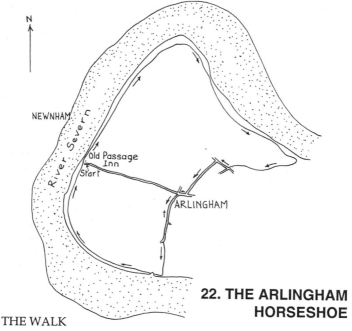

## 22. THE ARLINGHAM HORSESHOE

THE WALK

*From the inn go forward to join the path on the floodbank.* Your view of the river is going to vary, not only with the season of the year but the state of the tide, for here the river is strongly tidal. At low water vast acres of mud and sand banks are exposed, with the Severn running in narrowed channels. The incoming tide rushes in at a rate of knots with the banks being visibly covered as you watch; the hazards to shipping obvious to the most ignorant of landlubbers. The completion of the deep-water canal between Sharpness and Gloucester in 1827 must have saved not only time but a great number of lives, for many had died in these treacherous waters.

Immediately over the water is Newnham, the town looking especially attractive in the morning sunshine, with the parish church occupying a prominent position on the red cliffs that rise from the river. Behind the town lies the Forest of Dean and the Blaize

Bailey viewpoint from which walkers who have already followed the Newnham walk will have enjoyed the superb view of the Severn horseshoe and a wide expanse of the Gloucestershire countryside.

*Turn right, heading upstream, keeping to the floodbank for the next two and a half miles.* Ahead will be seen the spire of Westbury church, something of a curiosity for the tower is detached from the church and its shingled roof is said to have been made from old cider barrels. The occasional wartime pillbox still remains at the water's edge, foundations undermined, and like the memories of that conflict of 50 years ago, gradually slipping away.

As the bank curves to form one side of the horseshoe the long Garden Cliff defends the Westbury side. Beneath lies the oddly named Pimlico Sand, this lonely spot a far cry from the busy London area with which it may be supposed there is an obscure connection.

*Ignore the path which is signed off towards a group of farm buildings and continue for a full mile to take the path signed off right. The turn is easily identified; it is found 400 yards short of the obvious pylons seen ahead, at a point where a deep drainage ditch meets the river by sluice gates.*

*Cross the stile and follow a wide track with a ditch to your right. The track leads to a metal gateway. Do not go through but turn right and take the waymarked path heading westward over the fields for just over half a mile with the hedge line to your right.*

*The path meets a narrow lane. Here turn right, shortly passing Slowwe House, almost hidden behind its high garden walls. A little beyond the house the lane divides at a triangle of green; take the left fork. This is Friday Street, a pleasant lane edged with houses and farms, which in just under half a mile will bring you to the centre of Arlingham village.*

*On meeting a road junction turn right and in a short distance meet the village crossroads by the Red Lion. Turn left following Church Road for about 600 yards. This is another pleasant lane, passing the Old Dairy, and next to it the aptly named "Cottage Loaf". The church may be visited but, if locked, the board in the porch will tell of the Earl of Leicester's charitable connections with the village.*

*Follow the road until it bends sharply to the right. At this point go forward on a broad track which lies beyond a metal gateway. Soon a deep ditch is crossed and the track dissects the gap between the two great pylons that carry the power lines over the river.*

*Turn right along the floodbank which will take you back to your starting point after a mile and a half.* Along the grassy slope a distinct grey tide line formed by quite hefty logs and assorted debris marks the extended bounds of the river at exceptionally high water. The tree-crowned May Hill, 972ft, seven miles distant, is a feature of the northern horizon. Across the river lies a collection of boats tethered along the quayside by Collow Pill below Newnham. Seen through binoculars it almost appears as an extension of the cemetery and perhaps it is the ship's last resting place for the spark of metal-cutting equipment is clearly seen across the water. Have the *Arco Trader* and the beige single-funnelled *Freshspring* made their last voyage? Too sad a thought on which to end this walk, so a retreat must be made to the comfort of the Old Passage Inn for consolation.

## 23: NEWNHAM AND THE FOREST OF DEAN

| | |
|---|---|
| *Start:* | Newnham, on the west bank of the Severn 11 miles south-west of Gloucester via the A48. Car park by riverside on northern edge of town. |
| *Distance:* | 6½ miles approx. |
| *Detail:* | Riverside walk followed by steady climb to the forest edge with superb views. |
| *Maps:* | 1:25,000 Outdoor Leisure Map 14 (Wye Valley & the Forest of Dean). 1:50,000 Landranger 162. |
| *Toilets:* | Newnham car park. |
| *Refreshments:* | Newnham. Also van usually to be found in car park. |

Newnham stands on a low hill looking out over the Severn at the centre point of the river's great horseshoe loop between Epney and Frampton. There is a fine view of this reach of the river from the car park but its serpentine course is best appreciated from the higher ground of the Royal Forest of Dean.

THE WALK

*From the car park head up Church Road, passing Quay House which gives a clue to the town's past riverside activities, to reach St Peter's Church in*

# 23. NEWNHAM AND
# THE FOREST OF DEAN

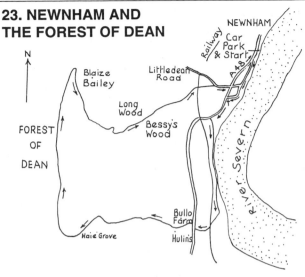

*half a mile.* There are excellent views of the Severn from the eastern end of the churchyard. The church was the scene of a skirmish during the black days of the Civil War. The confusion, and noise of battle, was considerably increased when a barrel of gunpowder somewhat irreligiously stored inside blew up.

*Go through the churchyard to avoid a dangerous footpath-less section of the A48. Beyond the church gate take the footpath along the road in the direction of Chepstow which is followed for about 200 yards. Leave the road, about 100 yards short of the railway bridge, taking the path on the left signed with the logo of the Severn Way.*

The full route of the Severn Way in Gloucestershire has been completed on the east bank, a 50 mile trail from Tewkesbury to the Windbound Inn at Shepperdine. The corresponding west bank is currently under development. The logo is not without interest for it depicts a Severn Trow, a shallow-draught boat especially designed for the difficult waters of the river. Although equipped with a large sail its progress upstream was mainly by man-power rather than the harnessing of the wind. Gangs of men, twenty strong, hauled the heavily laden boats upstream to the river ports which stretched far inland.

111

*This waymarked path is now followed southwards for the next mile, as described. Pass through a metal gateway turning immediately right onto a fenced track, passing farm buildings. After about 100 yards pass through a metal gateway/stile. After crossing a streamlet the path goes forward through a field with a hedge to your left and the Severn some 40ft to 50ft below.*

Sharp spiked blackthorn bushes edge the cliff, white-flowered in spring followed in August by blue plum-like fruit which unlike other members of the family do not mature until well into autumn. The fruit is extremely bitter. A wayside sampling is not recommended, but it found a place in the herbalist's armoury, variously prepared to treat a number of human discomforts including infections of the mouth. Today it is better known as the flavouring used in sloe gin.

Looking back upstream you will see the white-painted Old Passage Inn on the east bank at Arlingham, marking a centuries-old crossing of the river, now discontinued. An attempt to bridge the gap using techniques developed during the Second World War did not survive long against the battering of the powerful Severn tides. On the west side boats may be seen moored by Collow Pill and Newnham church in its commanding position on the red cliffs.

*A narrow but clear path follows close to the cliff edge and as summer advances small flocks of goldfinches may be seen here feeding off the thistle heads. The path widens to pass through a belt of trees with the railway on your right, a scenic route for passengers with long views down the river and to the Forest of Dean. Beyond the trees continue through a field, still with the hedgerow on your right, with further views of the impressive loop of the Severn as it starts to wind back on the lower portion of the horseshoe bend.*

*At the end of the field cross a stile which leads onto a track with a bungalow, Kindlands Major, half right. Cross the track to the stile immediately opposite beyond which lies a fenced path. From here there is a brief view downstream to the rust-red cliffs which jut into the river from Box Grove. Below, Box Hole is reputed to be 90ft deep.*

*After 100 yards the path joins a metalled lane. Follow this, soon leaving the Severn Way. Turn right over two stiles, at the top end of an orchard, to cross the railway. The line is in regular service so care is required. On the far side of the track swing left to meet a lane and turn right with it to*

Above:
Berkeley Castle

Left:
The Grove and
Mill Grove from
the old track
to Dean Hill

Above:
The old trackway
to Dean Hill

Right:
The tall ships
still come to
Gloucester -
The Soren
Larsen "star" of
the Oneiden
Line, in
for a refit

reach the main road (A48) after 200 yards by the sign to Bullo Pill.

Turn right and after a few yards cross the road to the track opposite, soon passing Bullo Farm. At a division of ways after 200 yards continue with the right fork, passing the ancient but now partially derelict Hulins Farm. Grass grows through the tarmac of this traffic-free old lane running between hedges and high banks, soon with a long plantation to your right beyond which lies Grove Farm. Here the tarmac gives out, but continue climbing steadily westwards along the old hollow way. To your right will be seen the buildings of The Haie. Continue to pass through a wooden gateway to enter the darkness of the wood.

At the top of the rise join a track coming in from the right and go forward, passing the grounds of Wanslark on your left. The track soon curves left, passing a derelict building and after a few yards meets a five-barred gate. DO NOT GO THROUGH THIS GATEWAY, but turn sharp left over a stile to follow a path along the inside edge of a wood. This is Haie Grove, the dark conifers edged by a lighter green ribbon of sycamore. A further stile is soon crossed with the falling path keeping close to the fence line. After 250 yards or so the fence and path swing to the right and in a few yards join a broader track coming in from a field. Turn left along this, soon to meet and turn right on a good track.

After about 30 yards leave the wood to take the right of way shown on the map which climbs the hill on the outside edge of the wood. (There is in fact a well worn path which follows the inside edge of the wood, named on the map as Gill Birch; both paths meet at the top of the hill.)

Cross the stile at the top of the hill to enter the forest and go forward for 40 paces or so before turning right on a slightly wider path which in a little under 100 yards brings you to a forest road. This is part of a Scenic Drive provided by the Forestry Commission. Turn right on the road which is followed northwards for a mile and a half, with a succession of excellent views.

The first of these is found after 300 yards, looking over the Severn to the western scarp of the Cotswolds, and below to The Haie.

The second viewpoint, found on your left after a few minutes' walking, looks out over the wooded valleys and hills of the Royal Forest of Dean with the little village of Soudley far below. Royal, since from Norman times the hunting rights were reserved for the sovereign and woe betide those who broke the forest laws. Today the Forestry Commission is responsible for over 20,000 acres of mixed broadleaf and coniferous woodland. There are many forest roads and paths open to the walker, serviced by numerous car parks, picnic sites and toilets. The long history of the forest and its people is told in the excellent Dean Heritage Centre at Lower Soudley. The museum lies off our route but a visit on another occasion is strongly recommended.

*Continue along the main forest road, with clearings providing a view to the hilltop town of Cinderford. In places conifers yield to beech and sweet chestnut, a tree said to have been introduced into the forest by the Romans.*

*The third viewpoint is found on the right, three-quarters of a mile on from the last stop and a little off the forest road. Look out for the small square of concrete (foundations for toilets that used to be located here) and signs that direct you to a narrow path through the trees, soon to cross a further forest road to the stone-walled and paved viewing platform. Here is the promised prospect of the horseshoe bend of the Severn.*

The walker looks out over the conifers of the Blaize Bailey plantation to the river snaking its way through the Gloucestershire countryside. The Old Passage Inn can be seen, a white dot on the far bank of the river. The river all but encloses the agricultural plain with its patterning fields unrolled like a great map. The eastern horizon is bounded by the Cotswold escarpment while to the north the tower of Gloucester Cathedral may be seen on a clear day.

*From this last viewpoint turn right, ie. southwards, to follow the forest road downhill for half a mile. Ignore the first track on the left but about 150 yards after the road curves to the right take the descending track on the left. From here on there is intermittent waymarking - a yellow arrow and black spot.*

*The track emerges from the forest by Blaize Bailey Farm. Here continue forward, passing the farm on your right. A semi-derelict house is shortly passed on your left to continue with the waymarked track passing through a metal gateway beyond which the track is hedged for a short distance. The fence on the left soon falls back and the way continues towards two barns seen ahead. The first is a fine old stone building with a tiled roof - elderly but interesting!*

*The barns stand on the crest of a hill in sheep country with a view to the Severn. Bear right as the barns are reached and immediately left as you pass the stone barn to cross the falling field to a stile directly opposite. There is another superb view of the vast expanse of the Severn in its course.*

*Once over the stile keep to the left side of the sweeping contours of the*

*The Severn Horseshoe from the Blaize Bailey viewpoint*

field making towards the corner of Long Wood. Turn left along the outside edge of the wood for a short distance to meet and cross a stile. From here head diagonally right over a hilly field to meet the north-west corner of a wood. (Bessy's wood on some maps.)

Cross the stile at the outside edge of wood and turn immediately left, (away from the wood) heading north-easterly with the fence line on your left. Go over a further stile at the bottom of this long field and continue to a stile on the left, part way down the field. Cross the stile following the bottom edge of the field and after crossing a culvert over a small stream go ahead for a few paces only before turning right over a stile to cross a small plank bridge.

Cross the field in the direction of the large house seen ahead on the hill. At the far side of the field go through a metal gateway to cross the bridge over the railway which has just emerged from the tunnel to your left. Beyond the bridge cross a stile and go forward, at first with a broken line of trees to your left which falls back by a small pond almost hidden under the shade of a large oak tree.

*The path climbs to pass between old walls to meet the Littledean Road (ignore the minor turning immediately beyond the stile). Cross the road, turning right to take the footpath which leads to Newnham's main street. Just opposite is Severn Bank, formerly known as Passage Lane which led to the ferry landing point.*

*Turn left, passing the Victoria Hotel, following the descending main street with its architectural mix of houses and shops to return to your starting point.*

## 24: ALONG THE GREAT CANAL - Purton to Sharpness Docks

| | |
|---|---|
| *Start:* | Purton, 16 miles south-west of Gloucester. Leave the A38 on minor road about 2 miles beyond the signed turn to the Slimbridge Wild Fowl Trust. |
| *Car Parking:* | Canal side opposite Purton church. |
| *Distance:* | 5 miles approx. |
| *Detail:* | A 2 mile canal-side walk returning by field paths which offer some fine views of the Severn. |
| *Maps:* | 1:25,000 Outdoor Leisure Map 14. 1:50,000 Landranger Sheet 162. |
| *Toilets:* | Next to the Berkeley Hunt Inn, Purton. |

The Gloucester and Sharpness Canal had a long gestation, over 30 years from its conception to completion in 1827. At the time it was the largest canal in the world and 67 years ahead of the Manchester Ship Canal. A tidal lock at Sharpness admitted sea-going ships for an uninterrupted 16 mile passage to the inland port of Gloucester. The flat landscape totally avoids the need for further locks, but there are many road crossings requiring a succession of swing bridges. The bridges open up to 30 times a day; the flow of traffic, much of it leisure craft which tend to sail in convoy, is facilitated by radio link to the bridgekeepers; a modern touch but the early spirit of the canal is preserved by the doric-columned porticos of their waterside homes.

From Gloucester, now the normal tidal limit, a further lock gave access to the Severn with cargo being transferred to and from smaller vessels to trade with the river ports further upstream. A canal linking Worcester and Birmingham was opened in 1815. The 46 mile long Staffordshire and Worcestershire Canal was opened even earlier, 1772, connecting the Severn at Stourport with the Trent and Mersey Canal being built at the same time. In the 1840s the weirs and locks of the newly opened Severn Navigation extended the run of safer, deeper waters for the 42 miles between Gloucester and Stourport. The early river traffic off-loaded their cargoes not to the canal boats but to pack-horses. Upton upon Severn was one such place, a barge port from which strings of pack ponies made their way over the Malvern Hills to Herefordshire and on into Wales.

For centuries "the ship of the river", the trow, a shallow-draught flat-bottomed boat equipped with sails but often hauled by men, worked the Severn; now the canal brought larger sea-going vessels into the centre of Gloucester. The enormous expansion in trade demanded improved handling facilities, Gloucester grew, and so did the docks at Sharpness with a rebuilding in 1874. The new tidal lock could admit ships up to 6000 tonnes deadweight and in the following year work commenced on the expansion of rail communications with an ambitious crossing of the Severn.

On a nicely nostalgic note it is a pleasure to record that the tall ships still come to Gloucester for refit in the dry docks of the Neilsen Company. Visitors to the quayside may see a tall douglas fir being trimmed to provide a new mast. As I write, the ship that starred in the famous TV series *The Oneiden Line*, the *Soren Larsen*, has arrived in the docks via the Gloucester and Sharpness Canal. She is back in Gloucester after a five-year round-the-world trip to undergo a six-month refit prior to taking part in the Tall Ships Race.

## THE WALK

*From the car park cross the swing bridge and turn left to follow the towpath for 200 yards to reach a second bridge and the Berkeley Hunt Inn with its colourful sign. Here leave the canal, bearing right on a narrow lane passing a small row of houses, one of which has a collection of garden gnomes and windmills over its porch, and further on another boasts a weather vane with a witch riding the wind on the traditional broomstick.*

*As the broad reaches of the Severn come into view note the first field to*

117

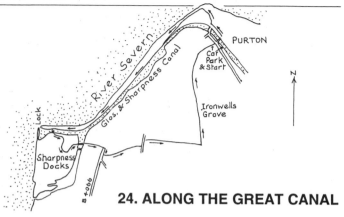

## 24. ALONG THE GREAT CANAL

*your right, a wildfowl reserve which provides winter grazing for geese who flock here in their hundreds, a reminder that the Slimbridge headquarters of the Wildfowl and Wetland Trust is only a few miles away.*

Continue along the lane to pass through a gateway, passing the Berkeley Arms. A walnut tree near the pub partially conceals a Second World War pill-box. A string of these were built along the banks of the Severn; many have been undermined by the river but a few remain as a reminder of the dark days of the 1940s.

Take the path which curves round the inn and on through a metal gateway to follow a hedged path which soon provides splendid views to the Severn and at low tide its extensive sand banks. On the opposite bank towards Gatcombe the river is bounded by the familiar low red cliffs. Here at Waveridge Sand the river has narrowed a little, three-quarters of a mile wide. Two miles upstream over the sands of The Noose the river is more than double that distance.

The track leads down to the river's edge with the banktop only a few feet above the muddy shores. A quarter of a mile from the Berkeley Arms leave the riverside by a gate to join the canal towpath which is now followed to Sharpness.

Initially there is a small diversion round the British Waterways quay with its blue-painted barges but a return is soon made to the canalside with only a narrow strip of land separating it from the Severn.

The riverbank here is a graveyard for the barges that once plied both the Severn and the canal. A strange place this, for many of these barges are of concrete, a recipe for a short sharp voyage to the bottom you might think, but then there was a time when some men thought an iron ship would never float. These barges were made at Gloucester. One still survives intact in the basin by the Inland Waterways Museum, concrete being successfully used as the submarine blockade reduced the supplies of imported timber. Not only the concrete barges lie here, their own grey memorials, but the decaying timbers of more conventional boats. These skeletons are a sadder sight, with their broken ribs. Shed a tear for the *Severn Collier* for she was made from the once living wood and will never again join battle with the tides carrying coal hewn from the dark mines of the Forest of Dean.

Further on beyond the opposite bank lie the old timber ponds, now reeded and a sheltered habitat for wildfowl as the noises off will indicate.

*A mile from Purton the hedge gives way to a stone sea-wall and soon the tall arch and round fortress-like tower of the eastern abutments of the*

*Not a castle but one of the remaining towers that once carried the railway over the Severn at Sharpness*

*former railway bridge come into view.* A remarkable feat of railway engineering, it was at the time of its construction the longest bridge in England and only exceeded in Great Britain by Scotland's doomed Tay Bridge which tragically collapsed in 1879, the very year that the Severn crossing opened to traffic.

The bridge, three-quarters of a mile long, was carried high above the river on a series of towers. In the autumn of 1960 one of the towers was hit by two oil barges, bringing down two full spans. Troubles never come singly and there was a further collision causing serious damage only a few months later. The single-track line was closed in 1965, the bridge demolished and the iron work salvaged for use elsewhere.

*The main waterway leads on to the docks with its warehouses, cranes reaching to the sky and the tidal lock. The towpath curves into the marina edging a long line of moored yachts and cruisers with names ranging from the mundane via the fanciful to the incomprehensible. Glass fibre is king here with only the occasional narrowboat, albeit devoted to leisurely pursuits, to fly the nostalgic flag of the river traffic.*

A plaque on a small white building close to the lock gates serves as a more potent reminder of our seafaring heritage and the part the Severn has played. It recalls that between 1939 and 1967 the Training Ship *Vindicatrix*, once a square-rigged sailing ship, prepared over 70,000 young men for a career in the Merchant Navy.

*Just beyond lies the old tidal lock but the canal should be crossed by the lock gates at the end of the marina. As you climb the steps on the far side there is an excellent photo opportunity for a long shot of the modern-day armada ranged along the quayside.*

*Bear left along a lane now with a fine view of the broad reaches of the Severn. Swing right at the water tower and continue to meet the road; here turn left. On reaching the dock road bear left and take the road which crosses a swing bridge, then a former railway bridge to reach the road, B4066, by the Severn Bridge Nursing Home, formerly a hotel and presumably named after the railway crossing of the river.*

*Turn right and after 100 yards take the footpath on the left following the edge of the field, with a hedge to your left and retrospective views of the docks and the Severn.*

*At top of the field exit by a gateway and head diagonally left on a well worn path to leave by a further gateway. Continue with the hedge on your left to reach a minor road by Malt House Cottage and turn left.*

*After 60 yards take the path on the right, following the field boundary (on your left) eastwards. Leave by the gateway and head across a large field, slight diagonally right, to a gateway at the top right corner. Continue along the next field towards its top left corner and leave by a stile on the left, a little short of the top of the field.*

*Once over the stile bear right following hedge and ditch and at the top of the field swing left (with the hedge line to your right) making for the stile by the clump of trees seen ahead - Ironwells Grove. Follow the field edge alongside the Grove.*

The modest height, less than 150ft, of this summit plateau provides improving views. First the higher ground of the Forest of Dean to your left and the Cotswolds to your right. Forward, the broad curve of the Severn and a glimpse of the blue splash of the canal. After harvest, when the agricultural cycle begins anew, hordes of gulls flock here to follow the plough, white wings fluttering in a great commotion over the newly turned earth.

*Continue beyond Ironwells Grove and after 170 yards pass through a gateway part way up the field. Turn left along the field edge to a further gateway and continue, with the hedge still to your left. Now the great sweep of the Severn is fully revealed.*

*Pass through a five-barred gate, with Purton village seen below. Bear diagonally right toward the village with the ponds of the water treatment works lying between the canal and the river. Head directly to the church which at this point is partly hidden by trees, your line of travel a little to the right of the power (or telephone) lines.*

*After passing through a gate head diagonally right to a further gateway and continue on the path which passes the church on the left to reach the road and your starting point.*

## NOTE FOR BIRD WATCHERS

Walking the canal near Sharpness one day in late November, amongst the birds seen on the Severn sandbanks were redshank, widgeon, crow, curlew, shelduck, cormorant, a large flock of dunlin, a solitary heron and black-headed and common gulls.

## 25: THE SEVERN AND BERKELEY PILL

| | |
|---|---|
| *Start:* | Berkeley town centre. 16 miles south-west of Gloucester, between junction 13 and 14 of M5, from where join A38 and take B4066 if approaching from north or B4509 from south. |
| *Car Parking:* | Marygate Street (currently free!). |
| *Distance:* | 4¹/₂ miles approx. |
| *Detail:* | Tracks and field paths lead to the Severn with a return by Berkeley Pill. |
| *Maps:* | 1:25,000 Outdoor Leisure Map 14. |
| | 1:50,000 Landranger Sheet 162. |
| *Toilets:* | Marygate Street, opposite car park. |
| *Refreshments:* | Berkeley. |

Berkeley is an attractive village a mile and a half inland from the rapidly widening Severn. Its claims to fame include the discovery in 1796 by Edward Jenner of vaccination against smallpox, in the sporting world the Berkeley Hunt, the construction of a Nuclear Power Station, and Berkeley Castle, scene of the horrendous murder in 1327 of Edward II.

The village sits comfortably around the church and castle but might have assumed a different appearance had the scheme for the Berkeley and Gloucester Canal been completed as originally envisaged in the late eighteenth century. Instead the intended course of the canal was cut short with the tidal lock and docks at Sharpness becoming the entry for the long needed safe passage to Gloucester for sea-going ships. The link with the Severn would have been made via Berkeley Pill, which forms the return leg of our walk. Today the site of what might have become a substantial docks area is overlooked by the Nuclear Power Station, currently being decommissioned.

This walk may be combined with a visit to Berkeley Castle with its pleasant gardens and excellent guided tour, the interesting village church and the Jenner Museum which celebrates his worldwide contribution to health.

## THE WALK

*From the car park in Marygate Street turn left, soon passing the Post Office where a plaque on the wall records that nearby stood the old vicarage where Jenner made his momentous discovery of the smallpox vaccine. On reaching the crossroads turn right into Salter Street.*

The town hall stands on this corner and reflects Berkeley's strong spirit of community. The clock was given by the villagers in memory of Nurse Buffton. The seat beneath it was presented by Captain R.G.W.Berkeley MFH and the village notice-board serves as a memorial to Tom Allen "... who voluntarily kept the streets of Berkeley clean and tidy for many years".

*Follow Salter Street leading on to Lynch Street for half a mile. After passing over a stream and under power lines continue to a curve in the road to turn right into the signed Hook Street. After 150 yards turn left on a lane passing Porlock House on your right. The lane soon becomes a grassy track running between hedges with Berkeley Nuclear Power Station seen over the fields to your left.*

*After half a mile pass through a gateway into open fields. Continue forward with the hedge line to your right and passing a large pond and after*

## 25. THE SEVERN AND BERKELEY PILL

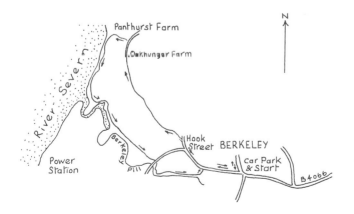

*a quarter of a mile reach a lane. Turn left following the lane past Oakhunger Farm and a further house which carries the arms of the Berkeley family.*

*Continue along the lane for 300 yards, then take the path on the left, found about 100 yards short of Panthurst Farm. Follow the field edge, with the hedge to your right. When the floodbank comes into view the path bears diagonally left to cross a drainage ditch by a bridge to mount the floodbank and join the Severn Way.*

The modest height of the floodbank provides views over the low-lying land which it protects and of the river which at this point is nearly a mile wide. Upriver are the towers of the dock buildings at Sharpness and the enormous area of a green-roofed warehouse. Across the water lies Lydney Harbour which once exported coal from the Forest of Dean. Beyond the harbour is a familiar red cliff, so characteristic of the river. A little upstream from Lydney explorers on the west bank may discover a putcheon weir, a great bank of cone-shaped baskets set in the river to catch salmon which are trapped by their heads. Downriver lies the huge mass of Berkeley Power Station and five miles on, the still productive Oldbury Nuclear Power Station. Ten miles from where you stand the 400ft-tall towers of the Severn Bridge point thin black fingers to the sky. These are all the works of man but closer at hand a startled heron rising in a small commotion from the river edge may attract your attention.

This can be a wild spot when a following wind blows up the estuary encouraging the conflict between the river's natural flow to the sea and the relentless surge of the incoming tide. It is little wonder that the churchyards along the Severn provide the final haven for those caught in the turbulence.

If the tide has ebbed the hazards of navigating these waters will be amply demonstrated by the miles of sand banks that occupy the greater part of the river at low water. Sainger Sands are almost opposite, running on to Lydney and Shepperdine Sands, nearly seven uninterrupted miles in length to the tip of Beacon Sand and over a mile wide at the broadest point. The channels between are narrow and winding, treacherous waters, the more so when the sand banks are barely covered by soupy waters, swirling thickly with silty sediment impenetrable to the eye.

*Turn left (downstream) to follow the floodbank for half a mile where it*

*The hunt in full cry - a gate top seen near Berkeley*

turns inland as it reaches the inlet of Berkeley Pill. Navigational light towers lie beyond the inlet with the Power Station now prominent.

Remain with the floodbank following the course of the wide, deep and tidal pill to reach the sluice gates in just under half a mile. Continue with the narrower but deep pill to your right. The Severn Way remains with the floodbank to reach the road in half a mile. (There is, however, a slightly more direct way currently shown on the OS maps. Shortly after passing over a culvert and through a gate the pill curves off to the right; a path, not visible on the ground, continues forward heading a little to the right of a barn seen ahead. Drawing level with the barn continue with the hedge to your left and after a few yards turn left over a stile to follow the pill, soon to reach the road.)

Leave the Severn Way at this point and cross the road to a driveway. Here, running along the top of a gate, is a hunting scene with horses and hounds in hot pursuits of the unfortunate fox. Do not pass through this gate but take the metal stile on the right, turning left to resume your walk along the waterway.

Ahead Berkeley Church and its separate tower come into view. In the distance is the tall column erected on the Cotswold escarpment at Nibley Knoll to honour William Tyndall on the 300th anniversary of his martydom. His crime?... the translation of the Bible into English.

After passing under power lines and then over a footbridge the pill curves to the left to pass the back gardens of houses. Soon you meet a wide track; turn left along this to reach Lynch Street, then turn right and retrace your steps to the centre of Berkeley.

# 26: OLDBURY NUCLEAR

| | |
|---|---|
| *Start:* | Windbound Inn, Shepperdine. Shepperdine lies at the end of a tangle of lanes signposted throughout from the A38 and is located on the riverside between Berkeley and Thornbury. |
| *Distance:* | 4 miles approx. |
| *Detail:* | Level walking looking over the Severn and circling the Oldbury Nuclear Power Station. |
| *Maps:* | 1:25,000 1132 (ST 69/79) or Outdoor Leisure Map No. 14. 1:50,000 Landranger 162. |
| *Refreshments:* | Windbound Inn. |

A nuclear power station and a country walk may not immediately present itself as a likely, or for that matter desirable, combination. Nuclear power installations and the more recent arrival of wind farms have found a place in the landscape which by their very size defy concealment and we have perforce to add them to the catalogue of the works of man that have spread across the landscape. Some remnants of past industry such as "quaint old watermills" we have taken to our hearts... others may not prove to be quite so acceptable!

In 1992 the 12 nuclear power stations then in operation provided around 15 percent of the electricity supplied to homes and industry in England and Wales. Whilst such stations do not pour vast quantities of carbon dioxide into the atmosphere there are other possible and greater dangers requiring scientific vigilance of a high order. Careful monitoring of the environment is an important aspect of the stringent safety regulations, with a continuous programme of testing samples of the atmosphere, water, vegetation including seaweed, soil and river silt, milk and fish. Oldbury has been in production since 1968 and in 1992 opened an excellent visitor centre with exhibits and conducted tours - no charge. This walk can be combined with a visit to the centre.

The previous excursions in the lower Severn area have all been in Gloucestershire but this and the next outing, which also starts from Shepperdine, are in the county of Avon.

The Windbound Inn shelters behind the floodbank, or rather the sea-wall, as it now seems more appropriate to call it. The Severn is

*Oldbury Nuclear Power Station*

tidal all the way to Gloucester and even beyond in exceptional circumstances. Walkers who have made a point of being in the right spot at the right time cannot fail to have been impressed by the great surge of water that sweeps upriver with the Severn bore (see useful information section). Looking directly north-west from the sea-wall to Grange Pill, the river is one and three-quarters mile wide. From the power station jetty only a short distance downstream it has broadened to two and a quarter miles. At the crossing of the river, four miles downstream, made by the Severn Bridge between Aust Rock and Beachley, the gap has briefly narrowed to just under a mile, but there is one more river to cross and that is the Wye, which is taken in the same great leap.

The tidal effect makes some dramatic changes to the riverscape; at low water vast acres of sand bank are revealed. The incoming tide rushes in with the river rising 12ft an hour. The walls of the tidal reservoir which serves the power station stand well clear of the river at the ebb; at high water they are lost under 20ft of water. Surely one day the force of this great movement of water in our river estuaries will be widely and effectively harnessed to supply power as previous generations used the rivers and streams to turn their mill wheels.

## THE WALK

*From the inn mount the floodbank and turn left downstream.* Ducks and other wildfowl are always present here. Canada geese will be seen, as will curlews, but it needs a slightly wild day to catch the atmosphere of the estuary. Seaweed hangs upon the barbed wire of the fences that lead down to the river's edge. Ahead is the Nuclear Power Station, like a giant double tooth or one of the those particularly magnificent cinema "palaces" of the 1930s. A flutter of white sails in the distance signals a small armada of hardy yachtsmen on the Oldbury Lake section of the river; the channel on the west side is less attractively named - Slime Road.

*As you reach the power station various notices request your co-operation in keeping strictly to the footpaths, warn of the dangers of the silt lagoon, and mark the boundaries of "... the Oldbury-on-Severn nuclear licensed site in accordance with the Nuclear Installations Act of 1965". You will notice the posts which carry material for the collection of air samples.*

Continue ahead with the hiss of steam from the power station mingling with the lap-lap-lap of the Severn waves, the plaintive call of the curlew now drowned by the hum of turbines. To your left the twin towers of the power station reach to the sky; here almost

## 26. OLDBURY NUCLEAR

OLDBURY

unimaginable energy is held captive within the heart of the reactors ... and to your right entirely without concern mallards happily bob gently up and down on the large flexible hose-lines that suck water for the power station from the reservoir. Prominent ahead is Aust Rock on the east bank of the river from which the Severn Bridge launches itself into Wales.

*Remain with the path round the station and continue downstream on the floodbank.*

*(NB: There is a possible short cut - a path leads off the floodbank close to the station which will take you back to the entrance not far from the visitor centre and connects with the full route. Take the path on the left along the edge of the power station boundary and after a few yards turn right and immediately left with the hedge on your left. Pass under the power lines and continue to meet the road by the entrance to the power station.)*

*The longer route continues with the floodbank for a further 600 yards, the Severn Bridge seen in slightly more detail with diminutive juggernauts, surely a contradiction in terms, crossing the long black spider's webb of steel hawsers and towers that suspend the bridge high above the river.*

*(NB: work to the power station has resulted in a footpath diversion as this book is being written. The route description which follows was prepared at that time but the presence of new stiles and some waymarking seems to confirm that this will be the permanent route.)*

*Leave the bank about 250 yards before the clump of trees seen ahead, turning left to follow a fenced path over fields, soon with a hedge to your left. A stile is crossed to continue forward with a drainage ditch to your right. Swing right for a few yards, still with the ditch, and then almost immediately left on a fenced path, crossing under power lines after about 200 yards. After a further 100 yards cross a stile bearing left through a metal gateway, over a ditch and swinging left on a wide track which after a few yards meets a road.*

*Turn left along the road, pass under power lines and after 100 yards turn right on a broad track met just before the yellow barrier at the entrance to the power station. (This is the spot where the link with the short-cut is made and the visitor centre is just ahead.)*

*Follow the track with a reedy drainage ditch on your left, a long straight lane with blackberries along the way ... but you might think twice before sampling them in view of the close proximity of the nuclear activity. We are continually assured that there is little danger and blackberries picked from a petrol-polluted roadside are likely to be less appealing.*

*After about 500 yards the track swings left, still edging the power station boundary, and after a further 500 yards bear right on a wider track for 200 yards to meet the lane by farm buildings at Job's Green.*

*Turn left on the rough track that passes the farm buildings and a hay barn on your right. After about 100 yards turn right through a gate and then immediately left, following the field edges to return to the floodbank by a waymarked stile. Turn right, retracing your steps to return to the Windbound Inn in just over half a mile.*

# 27: SHEPPERDINE - HILL Circuit

| | |
|---|---|
| *Start:* | Windbound Inn, on the riverside at Shepperdine between Berkeley and Thornbury and signposted from the A38. |
| *Distance:* | 8 miles. |
| *Detail:* | River bank. Old tracks and quiet lanes lead to a small hill providing good views. |
| *Maps:* | 1:25,000 Pathfinder 1132 (ST 69/79) or Outdoor Leisure Map 14.<br>1:50,000 Landranger 162. |
| *Refreshments:* | Windbound Inn. Shepperdine. |

The land lying to the east of the Severn floodbanks is pancake flat, contourless on the map, with the occasional spot height but a single digit. Deep ditches help drain the fields and were it not for the trees the landscape would in some ways be reminiscent of the East Anglian fens. In this territory even the most modest increase in height is noteworthy and this, it must be supposed, is why the tiny village standing two miles back from the river is simply called Hill. Buzzards hunt over this higher ground by day, owls by night, and deer may occasionally be seen around the wooded areas.

THE WALK

*From the inn the climb to the floodbank reveals the Severn, always impressive, and nearly two miles wide at this point. Downstream is the Oldbury Nuclear Power Station featured in the previous walk. Turn right*

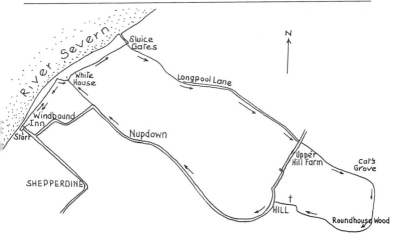

## 27 - SHEPPERDINE HILL CIRCUIT

*to follow the floodbank upstream, easy walking so that the life of the river can be enjoyed to the full with an eye to identifying the wildfowl and waders that may be seen along the water's edge.*

*In a quarter of a mile the sturdy stone-faced Chapel House is passed, later two light towers and then the White House as you continue upriver. Low tide reveals the vast acres of Lydney Sand and ahead on the west bank the now quiet jetty and tidal lock that gave entrance to Lydney Harbour where colliers once loaded coal from the Forest of Dean.*

*The Berkeley Nuclear Power Station, currently being decommissioned, comes into view as you continue to the sluice gates, reached but not crossed, a mile from the Windbound Inn. Here abandon the riverside, going forward to a gateway where you turn left on a wide track. After a few yards cross the drainage ditch and a little beyond turn right through a gateway, heading south-eastwards up a long narrow field.*

*At the end of the field pass through a metal gateway and continue forward, with a square coppice passed to your right. Soon the path divides; ignore the track which runs off right towards Dayhouse Farm. There is sometimes a large muddy area at this point but once negotiated continue along the hedged grassy lane, soon to pass through a metal gateway with willows to your left and a ditch to your right.*

*Remain on the track, Longpool Lane, which later becomes Stuckmoor*

Lane, which in a mile will bring you to the road near Brickhouse Farm.

Cross the road and take the lane opposite, passing Upper Hill Cottage to your right and continue on to Upper Hill Farm. Despite the name little height has been gained so far; the benchmark on the farmhouse wall is only 25ft above sea level. Go through the farmyard (dogs on lead, please) with stables to your left and house to your right. Leave by a metal gateway climbing through the fields, the hedge line to your left, and now with retrospective views to the Severn.

The south-west corner of Cat's Grove is reached in a quarter of a mile. Maintain your direction along the outside edge of the wood, passing through a gateway and continuing to the eastern corner of the wood. Here swing right along the short edge of the field (hedge to your left) and into the next field. Continue along the hedge but after 250 yards (there is a waymark) bear half right across the field to the gate at the north-east corner of Roundhouse Wood where there is a view to Newpark Farm perched castle-like on a hillock.

Enter the wood by a five-barred gate and continue on a broad grassy track. At a Y-junction take the left fork and after 100 yards leave the wood by a wooden gate. There is a good viewpoint here, over the Vale of Berkeley to the Severn and directly south towards Rockhampton and the ridge beyond on which stands Camp Hill fort, a mile and half distant as the crow flies. Turn right along the outside edge of the wood with the Severn Bridge in sight seven miles to the south-west.

The path pulls away from the wood, westwards over the field to pass through a waymarked wooden gateway. Continue forward on the outside edge of the wood and as it falls back a little make for the field corner to leave by a wooden gate. Immediately cross the footbridge over a stream running in a deep cleft.

Beyond a further gate continue forward up a slope to follow the path with the hedge line on your right. After crossing a stile continue forward with Church-hill Wood seen to the left, still keeping to the field edge.

The view over the Vale of Berkeley, Oldbury Nuclear Power Station and the silvered thread of the broadening Severn gradually unfolds as you advance. Continue, passing the plantation above Hill Court on your right. As the wood falls back the map shows a path continuing forward to descend to the road but swing right to descend diagonally to the church by a kissing gate.

The little church of St Michael's is a delight, well kept and full of

*Hill church*

interest; an inspection is recommended. In particular take time to read the memorial to Sir John Fust and his wife Dame Phillipa. It may cross your mind that behind the carefully composed words there lies the germ of a great novel.

*After visiting the church follow the drive down to the road and turn left. At the first junction bear right, signed Shepperdine 2½ miles, and follow the quiet lane to reach Nupdown, a small neatly kept hamlet where four farms keep each other company in an otherwise lonely landscape.*

*Continue along the Nupdown Road for half a mile and when this turns sharp left, leave it to cross a stile by a metal gateway. Go forward along the field edge with the hedge on your right. At the bottom of the field turn right through a gateway and then immediately left. At the end of the field cross a stile and bear left, passing the White House and light tower seen on your outward journey.*

*Head up to the floodbank and turn left following the Severn downstream for half a mile to your starting point at the Windbound Inn.*

## 28: SEVERN SPECTACULAR -
# Dean Hill and the finest view of the Severn

| | |
|---|---|
| *Start:* | Newnham, Glos. On the west bank of the Severn 11 miles south-west of Gloucester via the A48. |
| *Car Parking:* | By riverside on northern edge of town. |
| *Distance:* | 4 miles approx. |
| *Detail:* | After short passage along the riverside, field paths lead to an expansive view from Dean Hill. |
| *Maps:* | 1:25,000 Pathfinder 1088 (SO 61/71) or Outdoor Leisure Map 14. 1:50,000 Landranger 162. |
| *Toilets:* | At car park. |

For this final walk (the next is more of a postscript) a return is made to Newnham to follow a route that climbs by an old track to Dean Hill, which on a clear day provides from a modest height a wide and spectacular prospect.

The river at Newnham, as elsewhere in the tidal reaches, can look very different according to the state of the tide, seemingly undergoing a change of personality; at high water brim full, confident almost to the point of brashness, 600 yards wide at this point, always moving and sometimes choppy; at low water it seems to crouch as if trying to hide beneath its banks, now with its treacherous sandbanks revealed and occupying twice the area of the river. This is the time to bring out your binoculars to take a closer look at the birds that gather here to feed. Easiest to identify and very likely to be seen is the heron, standing stock still with head inclined, the picture of patience. Other birds are to be seen in greater numbers than the usually solitary heron; one grey November day I counted some 200 dunlin ranged along the bank.

Westbury on Severn lies only a few miles upstream and this walk could be combined with a visit to the quieter waters of the formal canal gardens of the National Trust's Westbury Court.

*The Severn Horseshoe from Dean Hill*

## THE WALK

*From the car park head upstream, at first on a good path through the picnic site, later rather more soggy, and then a head-ducking and winding way through trees. At exceptionally high water it may well be advisable to forget the path and walk along the road.*

*After half a mile leave the bankside path just short of the Silver Fox Cafe and turn right along the road. Just beyond the cafe turn left onto Hawkins Lane, soon passing a garden from which a gaggle of geese makes its presence known. After passing under the railway bridge the metalled lane comes to an end at a house called Rhossilly.*

*Pass through a metal gateway and turn immediately right along the bottom edge of the field. Leave by the gateway and continue forward, soon with a small stream to your right, to the end of the field and go through a further small field to leave by a stile, heading for a gateway seen ahead. Go diagonally left over the next field towards the cream-painted Wyncolls Farm. Beyond the stile take the path which at first edges the field boundary, passing the farm on your right, then cuts across the corner to a stile. Cross*

135

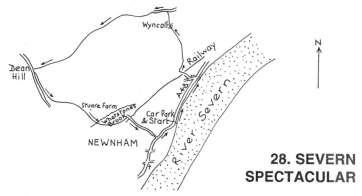

# 28. SEVERN SPECTACULAR

*a short field to the opposite stile and turn left into a lane.*

*After passing a handsome white house the metalled lane comes to an end, but with a bridleway signed ahead.*

*There now follows a long steady climb of a mile and a quarter following an old and excellent track, at times lost to the world in a deep hollow way or emerging to provide improving views over the Severn Valley on the left and to hilly sheep pastures on the right.*

*Follow the hedged and waymarked bridleway, soon crossing a footbridge where a stream falls over a small weir, with a pool hidden away in the field beyond where swans may be seen. Keep with the fenced/hedged path gated in places and ignoring the good track which heads off to the right. Morse's Grove is passed to your right and at a distance, the white-painted many gabled and beautifully situated house The Grove. Here it lies amidst the rolling green sheep pastures, topped by Mill Grove with its ancient earthwork. The more open aspect here offers even better views but the best is yet to come.*

*Continue climbing steadily towards another white-painted house, The Moors. Just short of the buildings go through a waymarked gate/stile, passing them on your right to join a metalled lane. After 60 yards leave the lane and go forward over a stile, climbing steeply over a short field to a further stile, then on a narrow path which after a short distance brings you to Littledean Road.*

*(To your right along the road lies Little Dean Hall, reputedly much haunted and said to be England's oldest known house - open*

to the public - see useful information section.)

You now stand on the slopes of Dean Hill, looking eastwards over the promised spectacular view; on a clear day it will not disappoint. Here laid before you is the great ten mile horseshoe bend of the Severn almost encircling the low-lying farmland around Arlingham. The little town of Newnham can be seen at the centre of the loop, with its cliff-top church which surely counted mariners as well as farmers amongst its parishioners. Over the river can be seen a solitary white building, the Old Passage Inn from which the centuries-old ferry crossed to Newnham. Northwards the detached shingled spire of SS *Peter & Paul* signals Westbury on Severn. Thirteen miles to the north-east the sun may spotlight the white limestone tower of Gloucester Cathedral and filling in the eastern horizon is the long line of the Cotswold escarpment.

Behind the walker is a cottage, Gazebo, built in 1749. What a superb view the locals must enjoy each day through the changing seasons. Not only the wide prospect of river, hills, field and farms but at times an amazing skyscape when great billowing clouds fill the heavens, and what a place from which to watch a thunderstorm!

## THE WALK CONTINUED

*From your viewpoint cross the metal stile and descend close to the hedge line. Toward the end of the field curve left a little to meet and cross a stile in the hedgerow. Head over a short field to a further stile to emerge on to the track which leads to Cockshoot Farm. Cross the track to a stile opposite and continue downhill (half right) to the opposite corner of the field to a waymarked stile.*

*Here, under a large ash tree, there are further good views to the Severn vale. Continue forward with a hedge on your right and after 300 yards (before reaching the end of the field) turn right over a stile and plank bridge. Just opposite, a large oak tree seems to grow out of the underlying sandstone rock. Turn left along the field edge descending to a stile seen ahead.*

*Once over the stile continue on, passing one of the barns of Stuare Farm on your left. Immediately beyond the barn cross a stile and turn right over a further stile, passing cow barns on your left, soon to meet and cross the farm road.*

*From the farm road cross the field, with no visible path, keeping the* power lines to your left - it can be a little squelchy in this area - to meet a stile. Here cross a bridge over the Whetstones Brook beyond which a seat has been placed as part of a Community Footpath Project.

Climb the bank by a stepped path to a further stile and continue climbing steeply and robbed of the view. At the top of the rise go forward to a gateway seen ahead with the houses of Newnham before you, the long straight line of the railway track half left and a more distant view to the tree-crowned May Hill near Newent.

Beyond the gate head half left over a field, now on a clearer path, to cross a stile by an old stone cottage, currently being restored. Here turn right and remain with it to reach Newnham by the clock tower.

Turn left down Lower High Street, with its interesting architectural mix, to return to the car park.

# THE SEVERN BRIDGE

This is not an itinerary for a walk but a suggestion for an exploration, long or short, of one of our more unusual public footpaths. On the eastern side of the Severn, near the M4 Motorway Services at Aust (where incidentally there is an excellent viewing platform from which to see the bridge and the estuary), a familiar green and white sign announces Public Footpath Chepstow 4 miles. A commonplace for the walker but with a difference, for the path which he is invited to follow crosses the swaying bridge high over the waters of the River Severn.

On one side the deep drop to the swirling muddy brown waters of the river, on the other only feet away the great rush of the constant stream of traffic. At hand the great steel hawsers that climb skywards to the tops of the 400ft-high towers from which the bridge is suspended.

The crossing is one that has been made in various fashions for longer than recorded history. Certainly the Romans must have used this narrowing of the Severn to link with their "Camp of the Legions" - Caerleon and their city of Caerwent. It was always a potentially dangerous crossing, one that has taken a toll of the lives of many ferrymen and their passengers.

Muscle power gave way to steam in 1827 - about 40 years after the practical problems of steam navigation had been overcome. A railway ferry opened in the 1860s, followed by the Severn railway tunnel further downstream, in 1886. Paddle boats duly put in an

*The Severn Bridge from Aust Rock*

appearance and the ferry continued to operate carrying cars, passengers, cargo and livestock until the opening of the Severn Bridge in 1966. Although usually referred to only as the Severn Bridge, the Wye is also spanned since at this point there is only a narrow neck of land between the two. Now 30 years on an additional bridge is due to open in 1996.

Your walk on the bridge, as far or as little as you wish, will be something of a small adventure, perhaps at its most atmospheric when the sun is fairly low in the sky, giving a great silvery sparkle to the river. As you follow the footpath on the downstream side from Aust, watch for the putcheon weir staked out on the sand-bank far below. Putcheon may be an unfamiliar word deserving of some explanation of both its construction and use. This "putt" was just one of many methods employed on the Severn to catch the king of fish, once more plentiful than it is today. Initially made of basket work, now more often in metal, it is a cone about 5ft long and a little under a foot at the opening and designed specifically to catch salmon. Hundreds of these baskets are incorporated three or four or five high, in a weir constructed of stakes and hurdles. The salmon who is unfortunate enough to be trapped head first in the basket has little or no chance of escape.

Half a mile downstream from the bridge, at Beachley Point, the Severn is joined by its sister river, the Wye. Both had their small beginnings on the slopes of Plynlimon; now united they flow on to be joined by the Avon and the Usk, then on to the Bristol Channel and to the great Atlantic Ocean.

# USEFUL INFORMATION

## TOURIST INFORMATION OFFICES
### (Note: some operate seasonal opening times)

| | |
|---|---|
| LLANIDLOES | Longbridge Street, Llanidloes, Powys SY18 6ES |
| NEWTOWN | Central Car Park, Newtown, Powys SY16 2PW |
| WELSHPOOL | Flash Leisure Centre, Welshpool, Powys SY21 7DD |
| SHREWSBURY | The Music Hall, The Square, Shrewsbury, Salop SY1 1LH |
| IRONBRIDGE | The Wharfage, Ironbridge, Salop TG8 7AW |
| BRIDGNORTH | The Library, Listley Street, Bridgnorth, Salop WV16 4AW |
| BEWDLEY | St George's Hall, Load Street, Bewdley, Worcs DY12 2EQ |
| WORCESTER | The Guildhall, High Street, Worcester WR1 2EY |
| UPTON UPON SEVERN | The Pepperpot, Church Street, Upton upon Severn, Worcs |
| TEWKESBURY | 64 Barton Street, Tewkesbury, Glos GL20 5PX |
| GLOUCESTER | St Michael's Tower, The Cross, Gloucester GL1 1PD |

# SELECTED LIST OF PLACES OF INTEREST

MUSEUMS, STATELY HOMES, CHURCHES, CATHEDRALS, GARDENS, RAILWAYS ETC.
Opening times are given as a guide only and may be subject to alteration. Readers are advised to check current opening times.

**Powys**

| | |
|---|---|
| Llyn Clywedog | Reservoir viewpoints, picnic sites, Bryntail Mine Trail |
| Hafren Forest | Picnic sites and trail |
| Llanidloes | Local history museum, Old Market Hall (Powys County Council). Summer & Easter week daily 11am-1pm & 2-5pm |
| Newtown | Robert Owen Museum, Broad Street. Mon to Fri, 9.45-11.45am & 2-3.30pm. Sats, 10-11.30am. |
| | Textile Museum, Commercial Street (Powys County Council). Tues to Sat, 2-5pm, June to Oct. |
| Welshpool | Powis Castle (National Trust) includes rooms devoted to Robert Clive. Opening times vary throughout a long season but generally not Mondays and not Tuesdays early and late season. Grounds 11am-6pm and Castle 12-6pm. |
| | Powysland Museum and Canal Centre (Powys County Council). Winter season Mon, Tues, Thurs and Fri 11am-1pm and 2-5pm. Sats 2-5pm. Summer season also Sats and Suns 10am-5pm. Closed for lunch 1-2pm. |

**Shropshire**

| | |
|---|---|
| Shrewsbury | Clive House Museum, College Hill. Porcelain collection, domestic life of the |

|  | 18/19th centuries. Open all year, Mon 2-5pm. Tues to Sats 10am-1pm and 2-5pm. |
|---|---|

18/19th centuries. Open all year, Mon 2-5pm. Tues to Sats 10am-1pm and 2-5pm.

Rowley's House Museum, Barker Street. Exhibits from the Roman city of Viroconium together with costume gallery, royal charters and pre-historic artifacts and items from Shrewsbury Abbey. Open all year, Mon to Sat 10am-5pm. Suns Easter to Oct 12-5pm.

Shrewsbury Castle - Regimental Museums. Open all year, Mon to Sat 10am-5pm. Suns Easter to Oct 10am-5pm.

St Chad's Church, Shrewsbury Abbey.

**Atcham**    Attingham Park (National Trust) House. Extensive grounds including deer park and farm. Once the home of Lord Berwick. Open summer months from Easter, Sat to Wed from 1.30pm plus Bank Holiday Mons from 11am. Grounds open throughout year dawn to dusk excluding Christmas Day.

**Wroxeter**    Viroconium, once the fourth largest Roman city in Britain. English Heritage. Open all year (except winter Mons, Christmas and New Year).

**Haughmond Abbey**    Substantial ruins. Open daily. English Heritage.

**Buildwas Abbey**    Substantial ruins. Open daily. English Heritage.

**Ironbridge**    Jackfield Tile Museum.

Museum of the River.

Museum of Iron Coalbrookdale.

Rosehill, home of the Darby family.

The Iron Bridge, the world's first.

Blist's Hill Open Air Museum. Life at home and work in the late 19th century.

Coalport China Works.

Tar Tunnel. Long open season. Check with Tourist Office for up-to date times.

**Broseley**    Benthall Hall (NT). 16th century house. April to Sept, Wed, Sun & Bank Holiday Mons 1.30-5.30pm.

**Bridgnorth**    St Mary's Church and Castle Walk viewpoint.

Cliff Railway.

Town Hall. Conducted tours of a most interesting 17th century building.

Severn Valley Railway, Bridgnorth to Kidderminster. Nostalgic steam 16 mile trip. Intermediate stations. Timetable enquiries (01299 401001). Services start early March (weekends) and expand to daily service.

Daniels Mill (Eardington). Working Water Mill. Open Sat & Suns Easter to end of Sept, 11am-6pm or dusk, whichever is the earlier.

Midland Motor Museum, Stanmore Hall, Stourbridge Road, east of Bridgnorth. Daily except Christmas Day.

Hermitage. Sandstone caves above eastern bank of Severn off the A458.

**Quatt**    Dudmaston Hall (NT). Attractive 17th century house and grounds. April to end Sept, Wed and Suns 2.30am-6pm.

**Worcestershire**

**Bewdley**    Bewdley Museum, The Shambles, Load Street. Lively and practical

|               | displays of local history. March to Nov, Mon to Sat 10am-5.30pm, Suns 2-5.30pm. |
|---------------|---|

Stourport     River trips in season, and the Redstone Rock Hermitage - see main text.

Hartlebury     Hereford & Worcester County Museum, Hartlebury Castle. Folk, costume, textile, children's gallery and horse drawn vehicles. Open March to Nov afternoons, Mon to Fri and Suns. Also opens Bank Holidays.

    Castle State Rooms. Limited opening, Easter to Sept, first Sun in month and Weds, afternoons, also Bank Holidays.

Worcester     Historic cathedral with tomb of King John. The Commandery, Civil War Museum, Mon to Sat 10.30am-5pm and Sun afternoons.

    Tudor House Folk Museum, Friar Street. Daily except Thurs & Suns.

    Greyfriars (National Trust), Friar St, April to end Oct, Wed, Thurs and Bank Holiday Mons, 2-5.30pm.

    Worcester Royal Porcelain. Factory tours (advance booking (01905 23221) and Museum, Severn Street (behind cathedral).

    City Museum and Art Gallery, Foregate Street. Regimental, wildlife and local history. Daily except Thurs & Suns.

Upton upon
Severn     Local museum with accent on the Civil War housed in the Pepperbox. Summer opening.

**Gloucestershire**

Tewkesbury     Tewkesbury Abbey, daily.

    The Old Baptist Chapel. A complete contrast with the Abbey.

    John Moore Countryside Museum, Church Street. Easter to Oct, Tues to Sats, 10am-1pm, 2-5pm and all Bank Holidays.

    Town museum with model of the battle of Tewkesbury, Barton Street. Battle of Tewkesbury Trail leaflet from Tourist Information Office.

Deerhurst     Odda's Chapel and St Mary's Church.

Ashleworth     Tithe Barn (NT), daily.

Gloucester     Cathedral with tomb of the murdered Edward II.

    Gloucester Docks, now restored.

    National Waterways Museum, Llanthony Warehouse, Gloucester Docks. Open all year, 10am-6pm (winter closes 5pm). Museum of Advertising and Packaging, Albert Warehouse, Gloucester Docks. Open all year, Tues to Suns, 10am-6pm plus Bank Holidays (closes 5pm winter).

    Regiments of Gloucestershire Museum, Custom House, The Docks. Open all year, Tues to Sun and Bank Holidays 10am-5pm.

    Gloucester Folk Museum, 99 -103 Westgate Street. Social, domestic and working life of Gloucester. Open all year, Mon to Sat, 10am-5pm including Bank Holidays.

    City Museum and Art Gallery, Brunswick Road. Roman mosaics, sculptures, antique furniture and art exhibitions. Open all year, Mon to Sat, 10am-5pm.

    City East Gate, Eastgate Street. Roman and medieval defences. Open

|  | May to Sept, Wed and Fri, 2.15-5pm. Sat 10am-12pm and 2.15-5pm. Transport Museum Bearland. Viewed from road. Horse tram fire engine etc. |
|---|---|
| The Severn Bore | The Bore, or tidal wave, can be seen from several points along the Severn including Minsterworth on the west bank and Stonebench on the east. The National Rivers Authority publish an annual timetable detailing the dates and times of the best prospects. NRA is located at Sapphire East, 550 Streetsbrook Road, Solihull, West Midlands B91 1QT (0121 711 2324). |
| Westbury on Severn | Westbury Court (NT). Water gardens. April to end Oct, Wed to Sun and Bank Holiday Mons (not Good Friday), 11am-6pm. |
| Slimbridge | Wildfowl and Wetlands Trust. Daily from 9.30am. |
| Berkeley | Berkeley Castle, April to Sept, Tues to Sun, 2.15pm. Oct Suns only. Jenner Museum close by. |

Printed by CARNMOR PRINT & DESIGN
95-97 LONDON ROAD, PRESTON, LANCASHIRE, UK.